Revised Edition

Collins

Knowledge Lighthouse

A SKILL-BASED COURSE ON GENERAL KNOWLEDGE

5

Seema Chari
Kunal Savarkar

Components of DigiSuite

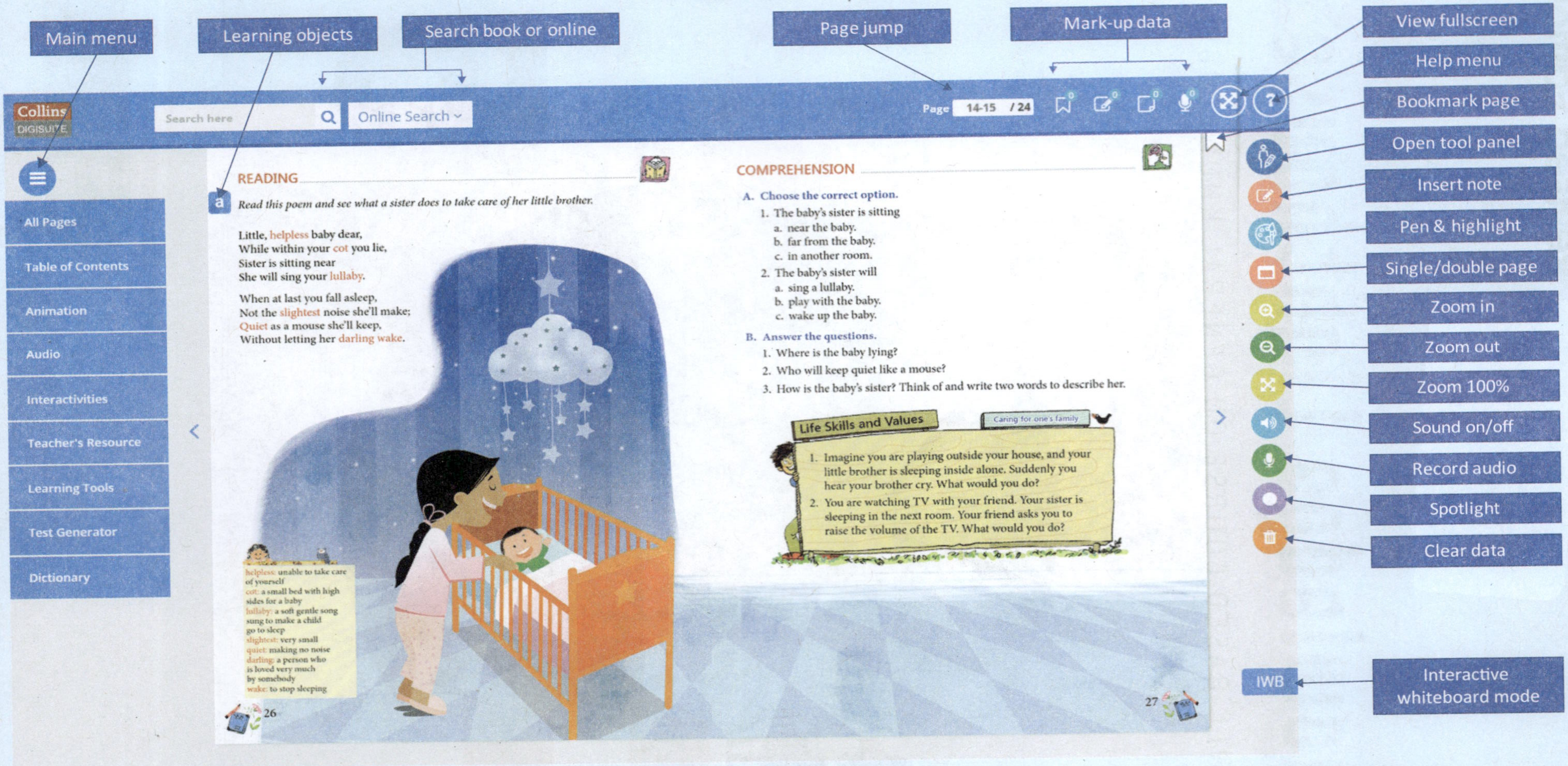

Student + Teacher						Teacher-only			
a	animations	**ia**	activities	**g**	games	**lp**	lesson plans	**tn**	teacher's notes
ilt	instructor-led tutorials	**w**	worksheets	**v**	videos	**w**	worksheets	**ak**	answer keys
		(audio icon)	audio						

Preface

Like the universe, knowledge, too, is limitless. No matter how much we know, there is always more to know. In the 21st century, thanks to the leaps that technology has made and continues to make, we shall have to gather knowledge throughout our lives; so much so that we have coined a new portmanteau, to describe it: 'upskilling'.

Another novelty of the third millennium is how we access and absorb knowledge. Apart from human sources (family, teachers, friends), there are the online ones (website, social media). Yet, despite all this easy availability and accessibility, it is not always easy to distinguish between real and fake, relevant and redundant, significant and inconsequential.

Knowledge Lighthouse Revised Edition is a series meant for GenZ, that is, learners born after Y2K. The series covers 'classic' general knowledge content for learners of grades 1 to 8, but lays special emphasis on skills —learning skills, literacy skills and life skills— as well as knowledge gleaned from new learnings of the past few years, from COVID-19 to sustainability, from data science to global issues in an ever-shifting, ever-ephemeral, post-information world. All the new chapters, although dealing with topics of great gravity, are presented in an age-appropriate and friendly manner so as to kindle interest and lay the foundation for more in-depth learning.

A critical component of the Knowledge Lighthouse Revised Edition books is the India content, wherein our country in all its complexity and diversity is presented through colourful, simple and exciting tasks, plus brand-new features such as state-focus, city-focus and visit-a-monument.

A particularly career-friendly inclusion in the Knowledge Lighthouse Revised Edition series is Science, technology, engineering and mathematics (STEM), the disciplines of the future, and new global issues, presented under World Today. We hope to lighten these subjects for students, by adding a little sprinkle of trivia to them.

Sustainable development is one of the key phrases of this millennium, but what does it really mean for us, especially for children? The all-new Life on Land and Climate Action chapters not only sensitise learners but also encourage direct and immediate action.

In the Skills pages, the life skills section has tasks on safety and self-awareness. Connecting the dots is the foundation of knowledge and the series has chapters based on Higher Order Thinking Skills (HOTS) and critical thinking to train young minds to see patterns, learn to eliminate or choose details and observe better.

Become a Champion Quizzer

Knowledge Lighthouse Revised Edition encourages all learners to be curious and explore the world around them. Those who observe and absorb all the time, learn from everyone and everything; they are the ones who become quizzers. Here are six rules that will help you become a champion quizzer.

1. Be curious—look around you, see everything, read everything.
2. Listen to others.
3. Seek out new experiences.
4. Learn to link events and people.
5. Do your own research and learn to spot fake news.
6. Remember, no matter how much you know, there is much more that you have yet to learn.

Now, go for it! We are sure that this series will expose a whole new generation of learners to the fun universe of general knowledge and enhance their love for learning and discovery.

~ Seema Chari and Kunal Savarkar

In this series ...

Knowledge Lighthouse tasks are thematic and linear with visual, verbal, and strategic inputs to help students solve them and acquire knowledge through a wide range of subjects and themes.

World Around Us

9 Breaking Records

Given below are places on the Earth that have one superlative feature: being the hottest place, the deepest point, and so on.

Complete these statements about the extremes of the Earth by matching columns A, B and C.

Column A	Column B	Column C
1 The Challenger Deep	a is the largest and most northerly national park in the world,	i making it the hottest spot on Earth.
2 The Caspian Sea	b in the Mariana Trench	ii is the world's largest lake.
3 On 10 July 1913,	c from Antarctica, the	iii is the deepest point on

World Around Us tasks take the learners on an exciting journey across the world.

Natural World

13 Adjusting to the Habitat

Solve the crossword to find the names of some animals who have adapted to thei

Natural World section uncovers the magical realm of plants, animals and birds.

Life on Land

24 Waste Not, Want Not

One of the biggest problems we are facing today is how to manage waste. So, we should not pollute the land, water and air with substances harmful to the Earth and its lifeforms.

Mark T for true and F for false for each of the statements relating to waste.

1 Polythene covers go in the

9 Use-and-throw face masks

Sustainable Development Goals sensitises learners towards sustainable development of the planet.

India Focus

29 Jaipur

Jaipur is the state capital of Rajasthan and its largest city. It is a UNESCO World H

Complete this brief essay about Jaipur with names from the help box.

1 Jaipur was founded in 1727 by .... He also set up the ...., which houses one of the five astronomical observ in India, and also has the Samrat Yantra, which is the world's biggest sun .... Fort, a fort near Jaipur is a UNESCO World Herit

2 An iconic monument of Jaipur is the five-storeyed ...., or Palace of Winds, which was built so

India Focus tasks are created to evoke a sense of wonder and pride in our nation.

Art and Entertainment

35 Indian Paintings

India has a rich tradition of painting and many styles have developed in different regions.

Find out the names of some of these painting traditions by solving the riddles.

1 My first is in MAKE, but not in CAKE ......
My second is in PANT, but not in PINT ......
My third is in DAMP, but not in CAMP ......
My fourth is in HUT, but not in CUT ......
My fifth is in BUT, but not in BAT ......
My sixth is in BILL, but not in HILL ......
My seventh is in FAR, but not in FUR ......

Art and Entertainment tasks celebrate artists, artworks, paintings, movies, awards and achievements.

Sports

36 Great Sportspeople

The names of some great sportspersons and their achievements are listed below.

Fill in the blanks with the sports that were played.

1 Sir Don Bradman was an Australian with a batting average of 99.94 in test matches, the highest ever.

C........ C........T

Sports section provides rules and records related to different sports.

Language and Literature

26 Roald Dahl

Roald Dahl is loved not only for his wonderful stories but also for the weird and wonderful characters he created.

Match the characters and brief plot in column A to the book in column B in which these characters appear.

1 Aunt Spiker and Aunt Sponge ill-treat their nephew who runs away in a fruit and ends up in New York.	a *Matilda*
2 A family of Muggle Wumps and the Roly-Poly Bird plot to punish a dreadful couple, and eventually escape after gluing the couple upside down to the floor.	b *Fantastic Mr. Fox*
3 Bruno Jenkins and his Norwegian grandmother decide	c *The Twits*

Language and Literature tasks present vocabulary and etymology in a fun way.

World Today

6 COVID Variant

All viruses change over time. SARS-CoV-2, the virus that causes COVID-1 changed over time

Fill in the blanks with words from the help box.

Changes in the virus means changes in how it behaves. Knowing these c help us figure out what to do to keep ourselves a .... from its effects.

What can change in a virus

- How b .... it spreads
- How severe the disease might be
- Whether vaccines or c .... will work

Word Today introduces the learner to the COVID and post-COVID world.

Whiz fact

Though Mount Everest is the highest mountain on Earth (about 8,850 metres), Hawaii is actually the tallest mountain on Earth. More than half (about 6000 met Kea lies underwater, while only 4205 metres is above sea level.

Whiz Fact is a spin-off fact about each topic or theme.

General Science

21 See a Specialist

There are many different types of doctors who specialise in treatments for different parts of the body.

Read the description of the types of doctors and match them with their pictures.

1 A doctor who treats disorders related to the brain and nervous system

2 A doctor who treats infants, children and adolescents for a variety of health issues

3 A doctor who is expert at treating many diseases and issues related to the heart

Psychiatrist

Neurologist

General Science highlights some scientific achievements and provides facts for others.

Whiz quiz

This popular sweet has many variants, but its easily recognisable avatar is a spongy mi ball swimming in sweet syrup. Thanks to the presentation and packaging of one Nobin Das and his descendants, the Bengali variety was awarded a GI tag in 2017 as the ...., while its yellowish-brown Odia cousin has its own GI t July 2019.

Whiz Quiz are fun activities that encourage self-learning.

21st Century Skills

21st century skills are necessary to succeed in the Age of Information. These skills are divided into three main sets, namely, learning skills, literacy skills and life skills.

Learning Skills

- Critical Thinking and HOTS
- Creativity
- Collaboration
- Communication

Learning Skills

2 Greetings

Here are some greetings in various languages. Read the dialogue below, guess what different words mean and choose your answer.

Girl: Hello!
Boy: Pleased to meet you.
Girl: Thank you.
Boy: Goodbye!

Spanish
Girl: Hola!
Boy: Encantado de conocerte.
Girl: Gracias.
Boy: Adios!

French
Girl: Salut!
Boy: Ravi de te rencontrer!
Girl: Merci.
Boy: Au revoir!

Arabic
Girl: Marhba!
Boy: Mumtan limuqabaltik.
Girl: Shukraan lakum.
Boy: Wadaea!

Swahili
Girl: Hello!
Boy: Nimefurahi kukutana nawe.

Japanese
Girl: Kon'nichiwa!
Boy: Aete ureshi yo.

Literacy Skills

- Technology
- Information
- Media
- Financial Literacy
- Data Handling

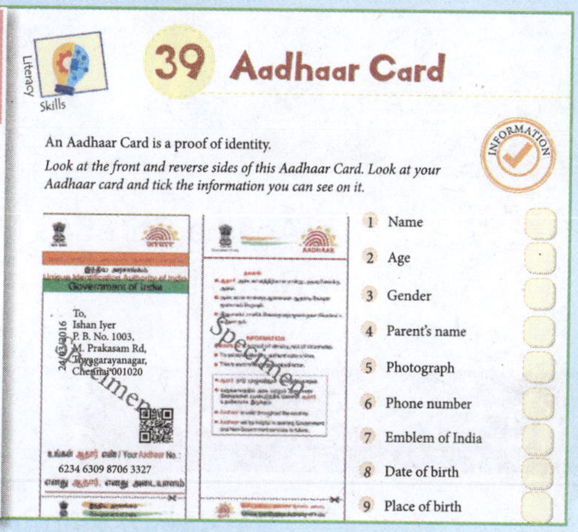

Literacy Skills

39 Aadhaar Card

An Aadhaar Card is a proof of identity.

Look at the front and reverse sides of this Aadhaar Card. Look at your Aadhaar card and tick the information you can see on it.

Government of India
To,
Ishan Iyer
P. B. No. 1003,
M. Prakasam Rd,
Thyagarayanagar,
Chennai 001020
6234 6309 8706 3327

1. Name
2. Age
3. Gender
4. Parent's name
5. Photograph
6. Phone number
7. Emblem of India
8. Date of birth
9. Place of birth

Life Skills

- Problem-solving
- Self-awareness
- Safety
- Social Skills

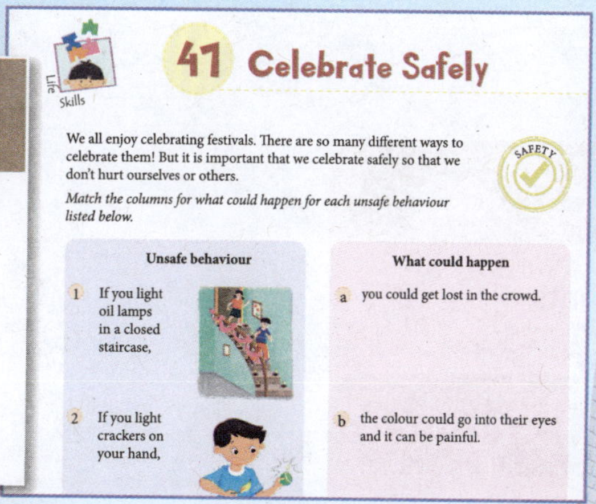

Life Skills

41 Celebrate Safely

We all enjoy celebrating festivals. There are so many different ways to celebrate them! But it is important that we celebrate safely so that we don't hurt ourselves or others.

Match the columns for what could happen for each unsafe behaviour listed below.

Unsafe behaviour	What could happen
1 If you light oil lamps in a closed staircase,	a you could get lost in the crowd.
2 If you light crackers on your hand,	b the colour could go into their eyes and it can be painful.

Detailed Contents

Contents

1 Toon Cross

Fill in the crossword with the names of famous cartoon characters using the clues given.

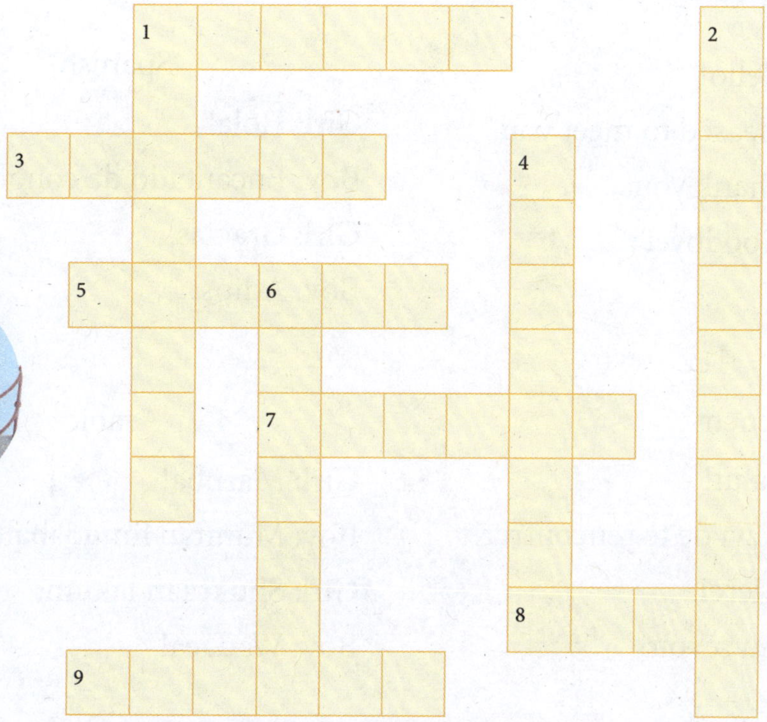

Across

1. Charlie Brown's dog friend in the comic strip called Peanuts
3. Spinach gives him superhuman strength
5. A high school hero from Riverdale
7. A perfectly adorable menace
8. A curious little explorer
9. The most famous comic mouse in the world

Down

1. A hero from the fictional planet called Krypton
2. The super heroine that Diana Prince becomes
4. An orange cat who loves eating, especially lasagna
6. A sea captain who has many adventures with his journalist friend Tintin

Whiz fact

The French comic Asterix was so popular that the first French satellite launched in 1965 was named Asterix.

Learning Skills

2 Greetings

COMMUNICATION

Here are some greetings in various languages. Read the dialogue below, guess what different words mean and choose your answer.

Girl: Hello!

Boy: Pleased to meet you.

Girl: Thank you.

Boy: Goodbye!

Spanish

Girl: Hola!

Boy: Encantado de conocerte.

Girl: Gracias.

Boy: Adios!

French

Girl: Salut!

Boy: Ravi de te rencontrer!

Girl: Merci.

Boy: Au revoir!

Arabic

Girl: Marhba!

Boy: Mumtan limuqabaltik.

Girl: Shukraan lakum.

Boy: Wadaea!

Swahili

Girl: Hello!

Boy: Nimefurahi kukutana nawe.

Girl: Asante.

Boy: Kwaheri!

Japanese

Girl: Kon'nichiwa!

Boy: Aete ureshî yo.

Girl: Arigatõgozaimashita.

Boy: Sayõnara!

1. Asante is the Swahili/Spanish word for 'thank you'.
2. Wadaea/Marhba is the Arabic word for 'hello'.
3. Sayõnara! is the Japanese word for 'please'/'goodbye'.
4. Salut/Hola is the French word for 'hello'.
5. Gracias means 'thank you'/'goodbye' in Spanish.

Whiz quiz

Here are some words from German and Italian languages . Guess their meanings in English!

Danke (German) .... Ciao (Italian) ....

Hallo (German) .... Dieci (Italian) ....

3 Spell It!

Use the clues and put one letter in each blank to find the correct spelling of the words.

Clue	Word
1 The day that comes after today	T ....
2 The murder of a famous or an important person	A ....
3 15 August is the day that India became	I ....
4 Essential, or something that fulfils a need	N ....
5 Naughty, full of mischief	M ....
6 Aware, or in a state to be able to use your senses to understand what is happening around you.	C ....
7 Practices to keep your body and surroundings clean to prevent diseases.	H ....
8 It has the days, dates, weeks and months of the year	C ....
9 Sure, certain	D ....
10 State of not being present.	A ....

Whiz fact

Words with multiple vowels or multiple consonants bunched together are often misspelled, for instance, vacuum, fluorescent, gauge, bureaucrat, and so on.

Natural World

4 Bow Wow

Many dog breeds get their name from the country or region in which they originate. *Use the image clues and description to fill in the crossword.*

Pomeranian

Irish Setter

German Shepherd

Chihuahua

Siberian Husky

Scottish Terrier

French Bulldog

English Foxhound

Across

3 This medium-sized sled dog is native to Northeast Asia; it is recognisable by its thick fur coat and erect triangular ears.

4 This dog originates from Germany and is known for its intelligence and strength.

6 This breed from Scotland makes a good watchdog and is very loyal to the family that it lives with.

7 This popular breed gets its name from an area located along the Baltic Sea in modern-day Poland and Germany.

8 This small-sized-dog is the national symbol of Mexico and is named after a state of the same name.

Down

1 This silky, long-haired dog from Ireland was bred as a hunting dog, but is also popular as a family dog.

2 This hunting breed from England has great stamina to gallop all day long and can chase animals by their scent.

5 This small-dog breed from France is a popular companion dog and requires close contact with humans.

Whiz fact

The Komondor is a Hungarian flock-guarding dog known for its natural guardian instinct. It is often called a 'mop dog' because of its white matted dreadlocks.

Life Skills

5 What's That Sign?

All of us should be familiar with road signs so that we can be safe on the road.

Use the help box to find out the meanings of these road signs and write them in the blanks given below the sign.

1 

....

2 

....

3 

....

4 

....

5 

....

6 

....

7 

....

8 

....

9 

....

10 

....

11 

....

12 

....

Help box

steep descent | pedestrian crossing prohibited | roundabout ahead | speed breaker | school ahead | falling rocks | no U-turn | slippery road ahead | right hair pin bend | speed limit 50 km per hour | dangerous dip ahead | one-way street

World Today

6 COVID Variants

All viruses change over time. SARS-CoV-2, the virus that causes COVID-19, has also changed over time.

Fill in the blanks with words from the help box.

Changes in the virus means changes in how it behaves. Knowing these changes can help us figure out what to do to keep ourselves (a) .... from its effects.

What can change in a virus

- How (b) .... it spreads
- How severe the disease might be
- Whether vaccines or (c) .... will work
- What kinds of diagnostic (d) .... are needed

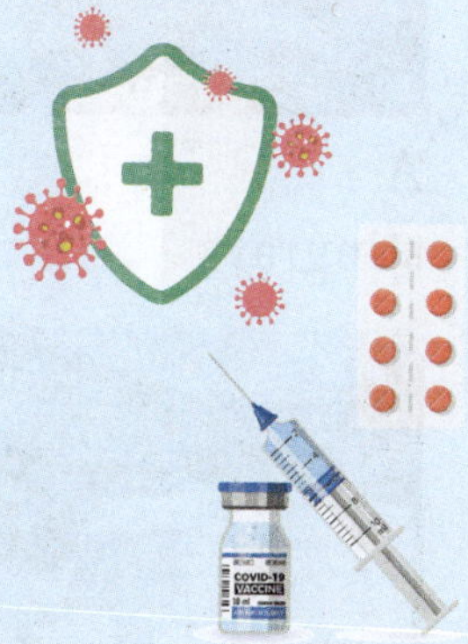

Since (e) .... 2020, the World Health Organisation (WHO) has been closely (f) .... the COVID-19 virus and its changes. These changed viruses are called (g) .... WHO's expert group uses (h) .... of the Greek (i) .... to name these variants so that you and I can (j) .... them easily.

Help box

tools	medicines	variants	understand	safe
letters	alphabet	January	easily	watching

Whiz fact

As of February 2022, WHO has named five SARS-CoV-2 variants as 'variants of concern' or VOCs. WHO is studying two more 'variants of interest', or VOI carefully; if they are dangerous, they will be added to the VOC list.

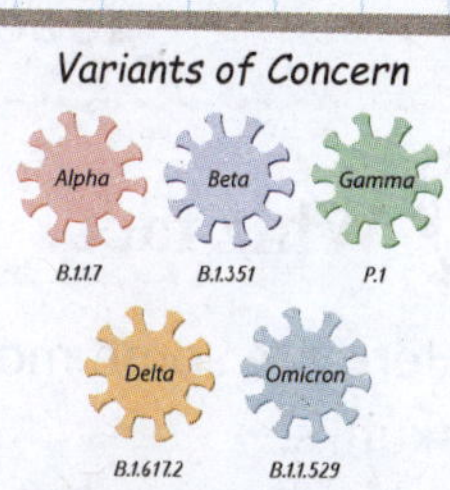

Language and Literature

7 A Pack of Animals

Many groups of animals have uncommon or even surprising names.

Use the picture clues and words from help box to guess the names for different groups of animals and write them in the blanks given.

1 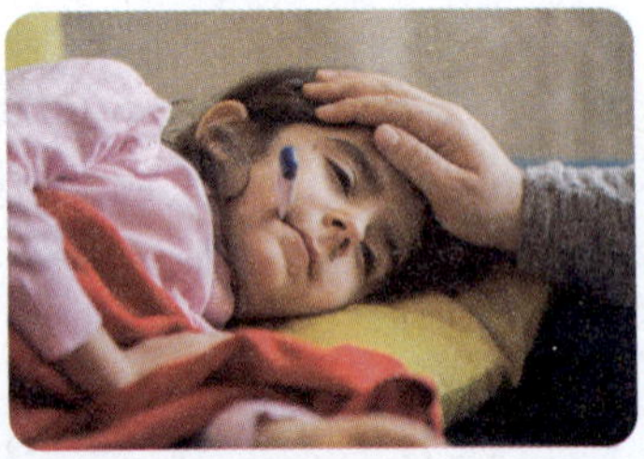

A .... of stingrays

2 

A .... of leopards

3 

A .... of giraffes

4 

A .... of camels

5 

A .... of toads

6 

An .... of frogs

7 

A .... of rhinoceroses

8 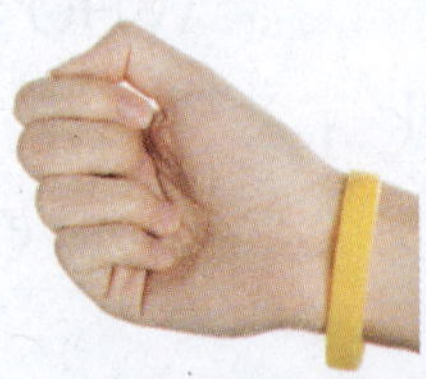

A .... of gorillas

9 

A .... of mules

Help box

band	crash	army	knot	leap
tower	fever	pack	caravan	

Whiz fact

Here are some more interesting group names: a shiver of sharks, a zeal of zebras and a stench of skunks.

General Science

8 Looking through the Light

If light passes through a material such that objects behind it can be seen clearly, the material is called transparent. Glass windows are transparent.

If a material does not allow any light to pass through so that the objects behind it cannot be seen at all, it is called opaque. A brick wall is opaque.

Say whether these objects are transparent or opaque by writing T or O in each box.

1 

Balloon ☐

2 

Stone ☐

3 

Thin sheet of plastic ☐

4 

Cardboard ☐

5 

Clear glass ☐

6 

Book ☐

Whiz fact

Some materials allow light to pass through, but not enough to clearly see the details of objects behind them. These materials are called translucent. Tracing paper, butter paper and frosted glass are translucent.

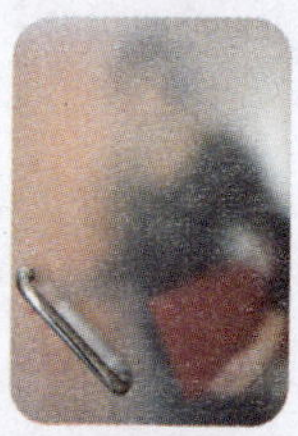

World Around Us

9 Breaking Records

Given below are places on the Earth that have one superlative feature: being the hottest place, the deepest point, and so on.

Complete these statements about the extremes of the Earth by matching columns A, B and C.

Column A	Column B	Column C
1 The Challenger Deep	a is the largest and most northerly national park in the world,	i making it the hottest spot on Earth.
2 The Caspian Sea	b in the Mariana Trench	ii is the world's largest lake.
3 On 10 July 1913, the hottest natural temperature	c from Antarctica, the nearest landmass,	iii is the deepest point on Earth.
4 Northeast Greenland National Park	d with a surface area of more than 3,70,000 km^2	iv is considered the remotest place on Earth.
5 Bouvet Island, situated more than 1,700 km away	e of 56.7 °C was recorded in Death Valley	v covering an area of 9,72,000 km^2.

Mariana Trench

Caspian Sea

Death Valley

Northeast Greenland National Park

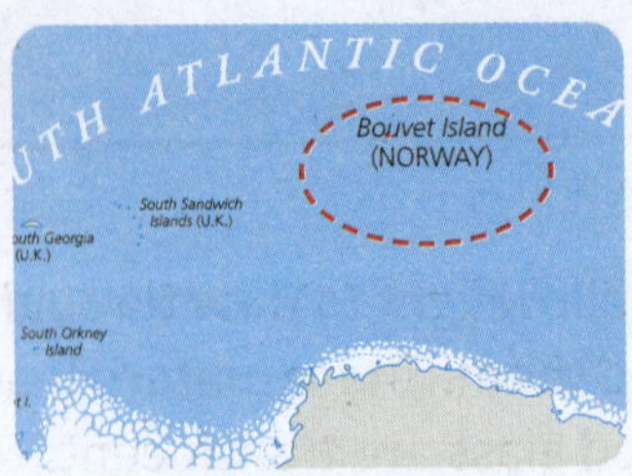

Antarctica

Amazon River

Dome Fuji

Mawsynram

Angel Falls

The Congo

Dead Sea

6 The Amazon	f became the coldest place on Earth	vi is the world's lowest point in terms of altitude.
7 The Dome Fuji in Antarctica	g at 423 m (–1338 feet) below sea level	vii is the largest river in the world.
8 Mawsynram in Meghalaya, India	h which discharges about 2,09,000 m^3 of water every second,	viii is the deepest river in the world.
9 Angel Falls	i with an average annual rainfall of 11,873 mm,	ix is the world's highest uninterrupted waterfall.
10 The Congo	j with a height of 979 m	x is the rainiest place in the world.
11 The Dead Sea	k reaching depths of 220 m in its lower course,	xi when the temperature dipped to –93.2°C in 2010.

Whiz fact

The driest place—the largely snow-free McMurdo Dry Valleys—is in Antarctica.

Sports

10 Olympic Symbols

A pictogram is an image that symbolises an object or an action. The 2016 Rio Olympics held at Rio de Janeiro, Brazil, featured pictograms for each of the forty-one events featuring in the games.

Look at the pictograms and use the help box to match them with their names.

Pictogram		Sport	
1		a	Badminton
2		b	Fencing
3		c	Boxing
4		d	Beach volleyball
5		e	Golf

6 

7 

8 

9 

10 

f Rhythmic gymnastics

g Synchronised swimming

h Sailing

i Track cycling

j Tennis

Whiz fact

The Tokyo 2020 Paralympic and Olympic Games used animated pictograms for the first time. These pictograms represented 22 Paralympic sports and 33 Olympic sports, each designed to visually communicate the characteristics of each sport and highlight the dynamism of the athletes.

11 Let's Visit Russia

Russia is the world's largest country. It occupies more than one-tenth of the land on Earth. Three-fourths of Russia's land is in Asia and the rest is in Europe, but over 75% of the population lives in European Russia.

Read the clues and write the correct answer using words from the help box. An additional hint that is more indirect and cryptic has also been given.

Clue	Cryptic Clue	Answer
1 The Russian unit of currency 	a It's part of the word trouble!	....
2 The largest cat in the world weighing upto 300 kilos 	b A striped animal, like the Bengal tiger, but in a cold place	....
3 This railway across Russia is the longest in the world 	c Named after a region that occupies more than half of Russia's landmass	....
4 The Russian script 	d This name is closely related to the Greek word *'Kyrillos'*, which means 'masterful'	....
5 This Russian river is the longest in Europe 	e Olga begins with a V	....

Clue	Hint	Answer
6 The deepest lake in the world with one-fifth of the world's unfrozen freshwater 	f Like a bicycle without the middle part!	....
7 This snow forest is one-fifth of the world's total forested land 	g Sounds like something to wear around the neck + sa-re-.......... -ma	....
8 A Russian ruler was called by this title 	h An anagram of a star	....
9 The official residence of the President of Russia 	i Rhymes with Gremlin	....
10 The national animal of Russia 	j You wouldn't want a hug from this one!	....

Help box

Rouble | Taiga | Baikal | Tsar | Volga | Kremlin | Cyrillic | Eurasian brown bear | Trans-Siberian | Siberian tiger

Whiz fact

Murmansk and Norilisk, two Russian cities, are among the northernmost cities on Earth. The economy of Murmansk is based on coal, gold and diamond mining, while Norilisk has enormous deposits of non-iron metals, including nickel, palladium, copper, cobalt and platinum. Excessive mining has put Norilisk in the list of the most polluted cities in the world.

Literacy Skills

12 Airlines and Logos

All companies have logos. Logos help people to instantly identify the company and its brand. Here are logos of some airlines.

Use the clues and the pictures to match the logos with the names of the airlines. Write the correct letter in each box.

1 

Air Canada

3 

Qantas

5 

Lufthansa

a The stylised peacock is part of the logo of this airline of one of India's neighbouring countries.

b The red maple leaf enclosed in a circle is the partial logo of this North American airline.

c This logo features Arabic lettering on a white background. The airline name is a part of the country's name.

d This major airline of India has half of the national emblem in yellow on a background of red.

e The flying crane symbol inside a circle is the iconic logo of this German airline.

f The logo of this airline features a flying kangaroo on a red background.

2 

Emirates

4 

Sri Lankan Airlines

6 

Air India

Whiz fact

Indonesia's international airline, called Garuda Indonesia, is named after the mythical mount of the Hindu God Vishnu!

Natural World

13 Adjusting to the Habitat

Solve the crossword to find the names of some animals who have adapted to their habitat.

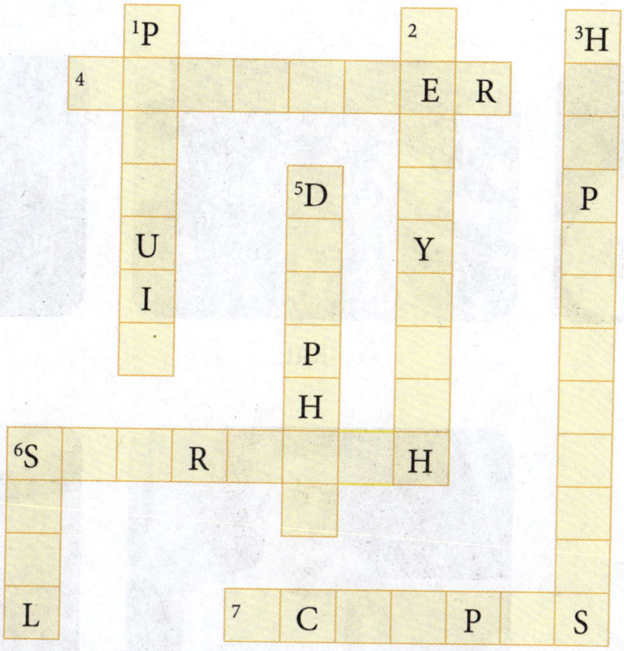

Across

4. It has wide hooves that prevent it from sinking in the snow.
6. Also called a sea star, it has no brain and no blood. Its nervous system is spread through its arms and its blood is actually seawater.
7. This creature does not have a skeleton, so it can squeeze through tiny cracks between undersea rocks.

Down

1. It is black and white in colour. Its feet do not freeze because they are covered with body fat and feathers.
2. It moves using its transparent tube-like hairs called tentacles.
3. A thick layer of fat under its skin helps it to keep its head above water and float.
5. It breathes through a hole called a blow hole on top of its head.
6. It has flippers that help it to swim in water.

Whiz fact

Antarctic fish make their own 'anti-freeze' proteins to survive in the frigid Southern Ocean.

India Focus

14 West, but in the East

West Bengal is farther east than Bihar and Jharkhand.

Look at the picture clues and fill in the blanks about West Bengal.

Sandesh

Kolkata

Howrah bridge

Hilsa

Satyajit Ray

Hooghly

Rabindranath Tagore

Darjeeling

Sundarbans

Bay of Bengal

Fishing cat

Eden Gardens

1 Rabindra Setu is the official name of the very famous .... over the river ....

2 The largest mangrove forests in the world, the ...., are in the Ganga–Brahmaputra delta.

3 The first Asian winner of the Nobel Prize in Literature and composer of our National Anthem was ....

4 ...., director of critically acclaimed films such as *Pather Panchali* and *Shatranj ke Khiladi*, was the first Indian to win an Honorary Academy Award for Lifetime Achievement in 1992.

5 The third largest cricket stadium in the world, named after a 'heavenly' place, is known as ....

6 The city of .... used to be the capital of India until 1911.

7 The part of the Indian Ocean from the Ganga delta down to Kanyakumari is called the ....

8 The Great Himalayan Railway, part of the UNESCO Heritage Mountain Railways of India, spans an 88 km journey from New Jalpaiguri to ...., a region famous for its fine tea.

9 Some popular Bengali foods are .... fish and sweets, such as rasgulla and ....

10 The Bengal tiger is the national animal of India and Bangladesh, but the state animal of West Bengal is the .... !

Whiz quiz

This popular sweet has many variants, but its easily recognisable avatar is a spongy milk-white ball swimming in sweet syrup. Thanks to the presentation and packaging of one Nobin Chandra Das and his descendants, the Bengali variety was awarded a GI tag in 2017 as the Bangla ...., while its yellowish-brown Odia cousin has its own GI tag as of July 2019.

Whiz fact

Bengal was partitioned by the British in 1905, rejoined in 1911, and split up again in 1947. East Bengal or East Pakistan became Bangladesh in 1971. West Bengal remains in India to this day.

Natural World

15 Disappearing Animals

Animals, like dinosaurs, that no longer exist on Earth are called extinct animals. There are many animals on Earth that are critically endangered, endangered and vulnerable.

Fill one letter of the alphabet in each blank to find the names of some critically endangered animals. Each letter is to be used only once. The only letters that do not fit are F and J.

1 CHINESE ...... AN ...... OLIN

2 CELEBES CRESTED MACA .... E

3 ORPHAN SALA ...... ANDE ......

4 TRISTAN AL ...... ATR ...... SS

5 SIBERIA .... R..... NE

6 RED-VEN ...... ED COC ...... ATOO

7 BALKAN
L ..... N .....

8 BLU ..... -THROATED
MACA .....

9 IND ..... AN
..... ULTURE

10 ..... AMA
GA ..... ELLE

11 SOCKEYE
..... ALMON

12 STAG ..... ORN
CORA .....

Whiz quiz

These are more names of some critically endangered animals. Can you guess the countries in which they are found?

Pondicherry shark: ....

Jamaican iguana: ....

Yunnan box turtle: ....

Whiz fact

Conservationist organisations working to protect vulnerable species have succeeded in getting the Panda bear, the Arabian oryx, the Steller sea lion and the Northern brown kiwi removed from the endangered list!

16 Agatha Christie's Mysteries

Agatha Christie is called the 'Queen of Crime'. In her lifetime, she wrote over 80 crime novels and short story collections.

It's your turn to play detective. Read the statements below and fill in the blanks. Join two words from each column of the help box to find the answers.

1 Agatha Christie created a Belgian detective named

....

2 ....

is the elderly lady detective who lives in a village.

3 The cases solved by the Belgian detective are often narrated by

....

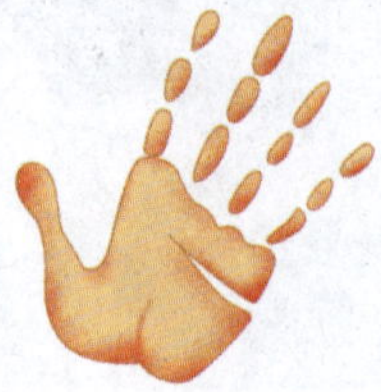

4 This apple-eating author appears in some novels with the Belgian detective.

....

5 *Murder on the* ....

is a novel where the crime takes place on a train.

6 The Belgian detective often solves cases simply by thinking, which he calls 'using his little

....'

7 ....

is a detective who advertises his services in the newspapers.

8 Agatha Christie also created a husband-and-wife team of detectives, the Beresfords, informally called .... (first word) and .... (second word).

9 The Belgian detective's secretary is called

....

10 ....
is the detective from Scotland Yard who solves some mysteries in the novels.

11 *One, Two,* .... (first word)
My .... (second word) is the name of an Agatha Christie novel based on a nursery rhyme.

12 This detective created by Agatha Christie is supposed to have been in the Secret Service.

....

Help box

- Jane
- Grey
- Tommy
- Colonel
- Parker
- Hercule
- Felicity
- Inspector
- Ariadne
- Buckle
- Orient
- Arthur

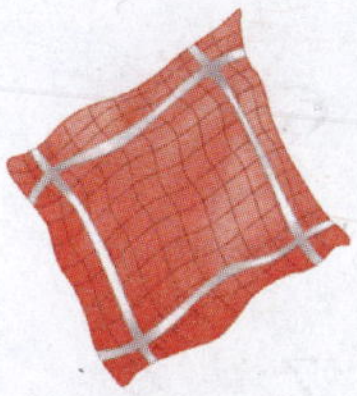

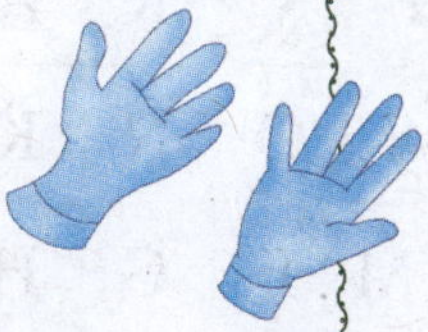

- Express
- Pyne
- Lemon
- Japp
- Race
- Marple
- Oliver
- Tuppence
- Shoe
- Cells
- Poirot
- Hastings

Whiz Fact

Agatha Christie also wrote the play *The Mousetrap*, which holds the world record for the longest running play ever.

India Focus

17 Holidays in the Hills

The blazing heat of summer eases when we think of summer vacations in the cool hills.

Read the clues and use the help box to find the names of hill stations hidden in this grid. Then choose the correct number of the hill station from the grid and write it in the box.

P	U	A	W	N	I	R	E	K	I	D	A	[8]M	[4]D
[10]M	P	A	V	G	Q	[11]G	U	L	M	A	R	G	A
U	B	A	T	N	U	O	[2]M	V	[5]P	K	F	J	R
N	Z	R	U	V	R	V	G	A	E	F	G	S	J
[7]N	Y	T	O	[1]O	V	P	C	G	A	K	L	[3]M	E
A	A	Y	E	U	E	H	I	S	T	L	A	N	E
R	D	I	Q	A	M	E	E	I	I	T	A	G	L
T	C	J	N	A	V	E	C	H	H	C	U	P	I
S	V	A	R	I	W	Q	I	E	Y	K	B	[6]M	N
D	P	H	T	M	T	N	R	O	R	Q	Y	A	G
V	I	G	T	V	R	A	N	P	O	S	A	N	O
B	O	B	W	O	N	K	L	F	Z	W	T	A	Z
U	E	Q	[12]M	E	G	H	U	P	O	A	G	L	J
J	A	[9]S	A	P	U	T	A	R	A	Y	R	I	H

A This hill station gives Haryana its tourism logo—the peafowl.

B Go further uphill into Himachal Pradesh from Kullu to find this hill station.

C This is the only hill station in Gujarat.

D Known for its tea plantations, this hill station is in Kerala.

E Located in Tamil Nadu, it is called the Queen of the Nilgiris.

F This hill station is named by combining the words for eye and lake.

G It is the only hill station in Rajasthan.

H This hill station in Madhya Pradesh is called the Queen of the Satpuras.

I No vehicles are allowed in this hill station in Maharashtra.

J This hill station in the Western Ghats in Karnataka is also known as Mercara.

K You can see Kanchenjunga from this hill station in West Bengal.

L Located in Kashmir, its name means 'meadow of flowers'.

Help box

Nainital	Madikeri	Manali	Ooty	Munnar	Mount Abu
Pachmarhi	Gulmarg	Saputara	Matheran	Darjeeling	Morni Hills

Whiz fact

Nestled in the Palani Hills in Tamil Nadu, Kodaikanal literally translates to 'gift of the forest'. Places to visit are the Kodai Lake and Guna caves.

18 Forceful Phenomena

Many dramatic and forceful events occur in nature. We often think of these phenomena as natural disasters. Do you know what they are?

Match the clues and the phenomena across the three columns.

Clue 1	Phenomenon	Clue 2
1 This happens when water overflows the banks of a river or a dam, or when there is excess rain.	a Earthquake	i Hawaii, Mount Fuji and Iceland are all examples of this.
2 This happens very often in Japan.	b Flood	ii So buildings here are built in such a manner that they won't collapse when this occurs.
3 This natural disaster occurs in the ocean. It is characterised by strong winds.	c Volcano	iii In the centre is a calm region called the eye.
4 This word comes from the Roman god of fire.	d Cyclone	iv To be safe, one should go to the highest point of land one can reach.

5 This rapid spinning column of air is among the fastest winds on Earth.	e Lightning	v If it lasts for a long time, it can cause famine.
6 This happens when there is very little or no rain.	f Tsunami	vi It is accompanied by thunder.
7 This huge wave like a wall of water gets its name from the Japanese word for 'harbour wave'.	g Tornado	vii In December 2004, this disastrous wave in the Indian Ocean killed over 1,00,000 people.
8 This appears as a bright flash of light in the sky.	h Drought	viii It is sometimes called a twister.

Whiz fact

A blizzard is a severe snowstorm that can last for at least three hours. A ground blizzard is when loose snow on the ground is lifted and blown by strong winds.

Sports

19 Which Game Is It?

Sports are more fun to play when you know their terms and rules.

Look at the pictures below and write the name of the sport these terms and rules are associated with. The name of sport may be used more than once. One of these is a fictional sport invented by author JK Rowling. Can you guess which one?

Lawn tennis

Hockey

Golf

Football

Basketball

Badminton

Table tennis

Quidditch

Each of the sentences below is a rule of one of the above games. Two rules of each game have been given. Write the name of the sport alongside the rule.

1 This game is not played with a ball. ....

2 There are 3 ring-shaped goals of different heights on each of the two sides of the field. ....

3 This game is divided into two halves of 45 minutes each. ....

4 This game may be played on grass, clay, synthetic turf or even concrete. ....

5 This game has a 'field' and an 'ice' variants, played with a ball and puck respectively. ....

6 In this game, players use many different kinds of clubs to hit a ball into various holes. ....

7 The top of the net must be 15.25 cm throughout its length above the playing surface. ....

8 Each team must have maximum of five players at any given time in this game. ....

9 If both players score 40 points, it is called a 'deuce'.

....

10 Only goalkeepers are allowed to touch the ball with any part of their arm.

....

11 This game ends when a Seeker catches the Golden Snitch and earns their team 150 points. ....

12 A match of the 'field' variety of this game is divided into two halves of 35 minutes each. ....

13 This game is played on a course, which occupies, on an average, 74 acres of land. ....

14 A successful free throw attempt counts as one point.

....

15 The ball is struck with a racquet, also called a bat or a paddle.

....

16 While serving, players stand inside the service court.

....

Whiz fact

The first tennis racquets had animal guts as strings. Today, they are strung with synthetic fibre, usually nylon.

20 National Flags

A flag helps you instantly identify the country to which a team, vehicle or building belongs.

Use the clues to match the flags with their descriptions and write the correct letters in the boxes.

1  ☐

2  ☐

3  ☐

4  ☐

5  ☐

6  ☐

7  ☐

8  ☐

9  ☐

10  ☐

a Dominica's flag features a purple parrot.

b Somalia's flag has a white star.

c Bhutan's flag has a dragon on it.

d The flag of Cyprus features the map of the country with two olive branches under it.

e Bahrain's flag has a saw toothed line between its two colours.

f The flag of Georgia features five red crosses.

g Nepal is the only country in the world whose national flag is not rectangular.

h Sri Lanka's flag features a gold lion holding a sword.

i Uganda's flag features a grey crowned crane in the centre.

j The flag of Barbados features a trident.

Whiz fact

The complex flag of Belize has the country's coat of arms on it, featuring a mahogany tree, two workers, a shield and a scroll with a Latin inscription.

Science

21 See a Specialist

There are many different types of doctors who specialise in treatments for different parts of the body.
Read the description of the types of doctors and match them with their pictures. Fill in the blanks with their correct names.

Psychiatrist

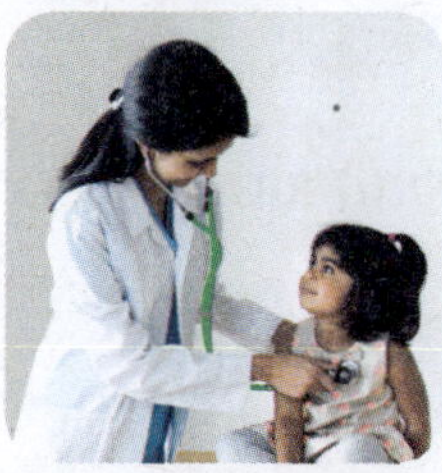
Paediatrician

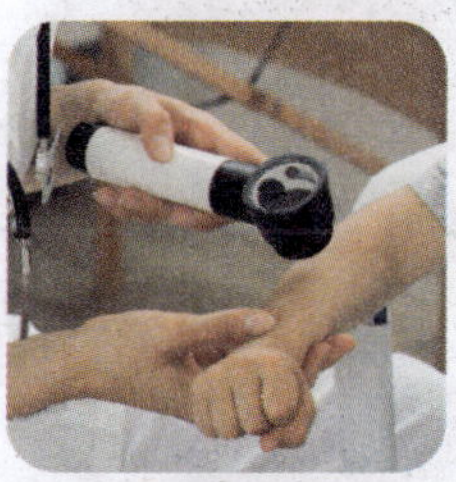
Dermatologist

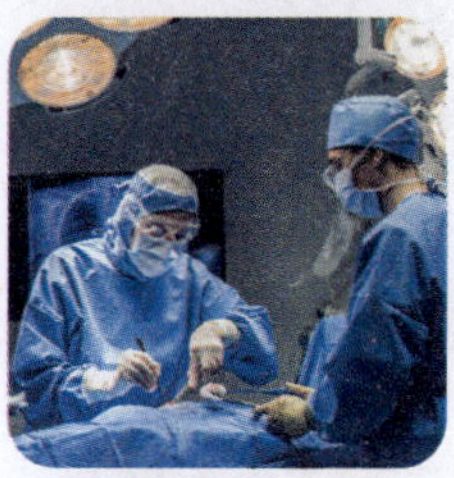
Surgeon

1. A doctor who treats disorders related to the brain and nervous system ....
2. A doctor who treats infants, children and adolescents for a variety of health issues ....
3. A doctor who is expert at treating many diseases and issues related to the heart ....
4. A doctor who specialises in treating patients with mental illness and behavioural disorders ....
5. A doctor who works with the human mouth, teeth and gums, and treats ailments related to them ....
6. A doctor who performs a wide variety of operations from the head to the feet ....
7. A doctor who treats eye defects, injuries and diseases ....
8. A doctor who treats diseases related to the skin ....

Neurologist

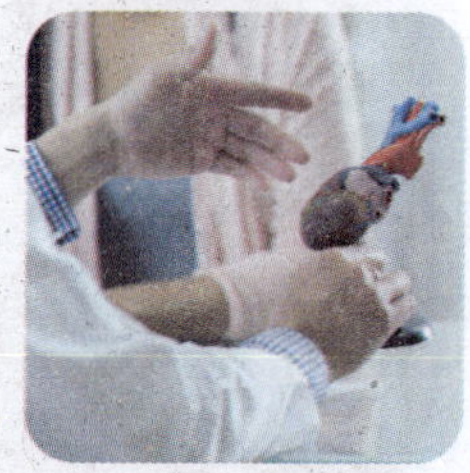
Cardiologist

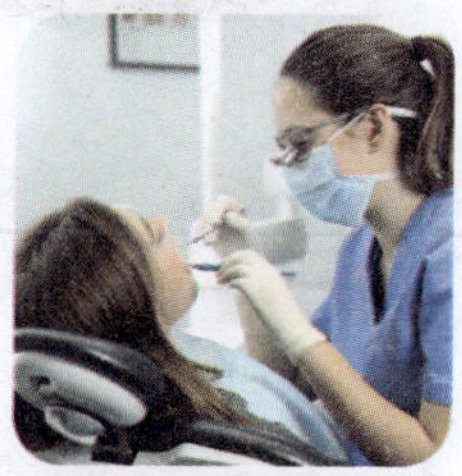
Dentist

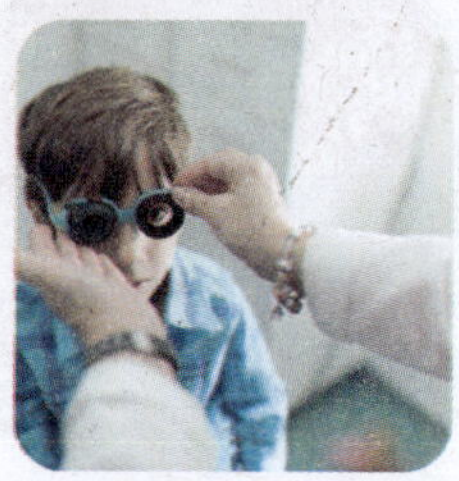
Ophthalmologist

Whiz fact

The anaesthesiologist administers anaesthesia which numbs the patient to pain. This is why an anaesthesiologist has to be present at every surgery.

India

Focus

22 Traditional Foods of India

India's diversity can be seen from its clothing, festivals, flora and fauna and delicious food. It is said that the flavour of the food changes with every 100 kilometres you travel in India.

Use the help box to identify the states to which these traditional foods belong and write their names in the blanks given.

1. *Yakhni* is a curry dish in which mutton or vegetable is cooked in spices, curd and saffron.

   ....

2. *Dal bati churma* is spicy *dal* with sweet *churma* along with deep fried crunchy *batis*.

   ....

3. *Xit Codi* is tangy fish curry served with steamed rice.

   ....

4. *Bisi bele bath* is a dish in which *sambar dal* and rice are cooked together with tamarind and spice powders.

   ....

5. *Dham* is a feast that includes rice. *rajma, dal,* vegetable curry and a sweet dish.

   ....

6 *Litti* is baked from wheat flour that is stuffed with a mixture of roasted gram flour, spices and lemon juice, served with *chokha*, which is pulped and cooked vegetables.

....

7 *Papaya khar* is a combination of red rice, beaten pulses and raw papaya along with traditional regional spices.

....

8 *Makke di roti* and *sarson da saag* is a dish comprising flatbread made of corn and slow-cooked mustard greens.

....

9 *Misal pav* is a water-based curried preparation of cooked sprouted lentils served with *pav* (bread rolls).

....

Help box

Assam	Maharashtra	Bihar	Himachal Pradesh
Goa	Kashmir	Rajasthan	Punjab	Karnataka

Whiz fact

India is called the land of spices. No country in the world produces as many varieties of spices as India.

23 Around the World

Here are a number of statements that will take you around the world. Match the two halves of each statement.

1 The Kalahari, Gobi and Atacama

a are also known as the Southern Lights.

2 The Isthmus of Panama

b are all deserts.

3 The Cape of Good Hope

c are mountain ranges in Europe.

4 The Jura, Pyrenees and Dolomites

d joins North America with South America.

5 Aurora Australis

e is at the southern tip of Africa.

6 The Tropic of Cancer and the Tropic of Capricorn

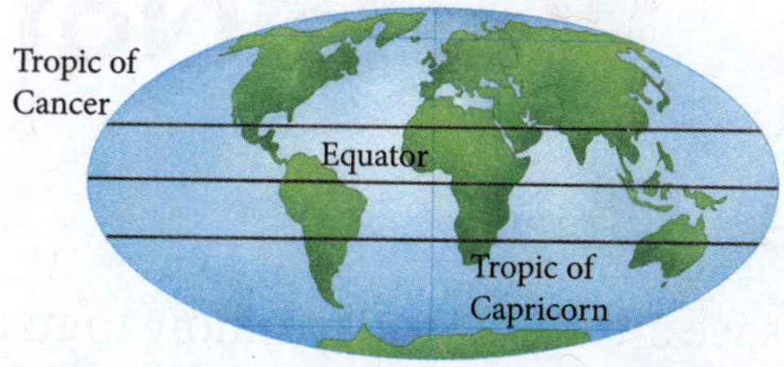

f is below the Atlantic Ocean.

7 The Bay of Bengal, Indian Ocean and the Arabian Sea

g both pass through Africa.

8 Puerto Rico, Tonga and Mariana

h is in Indonesia.

9 The biggest archipelago in the world

i are three water bodies surrounding India.

10 The longest mountain range in the world

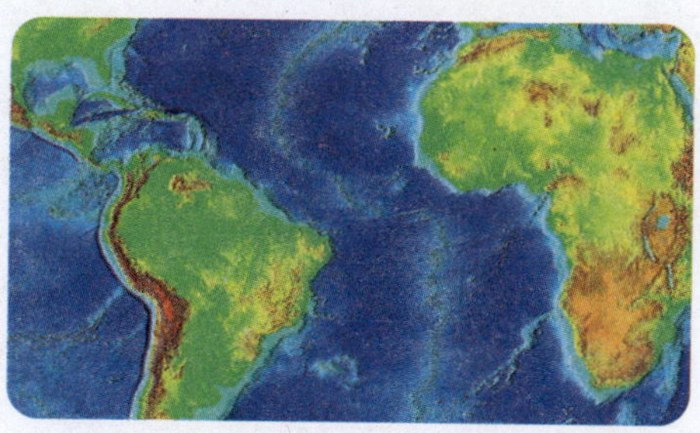

j are all names of ocean trenches.

Whiz fact

Though Mount Everest is the highest mountain on Earth (about 8,850 metres), Mount Kea in Hawaii is actually the tallest mountain on Earth. More than half (about 6000 metres) of Mount Kea lies underwater, while only 4205 metres is above sea level.

24 Waste Not, Want Not

One of the biggest problems we are facing today is how to manage waste. So, we should not pollute the land, water and air with substances harmful to the Earth and its lifeforms.

Mark T for true and F for false for each of the statements relating to waste.

1. Polythene covers go in the recycle bin. ☐
2. Fruit peels go in the compost bin. ☐
3. Bulbs go in the e-waste bin. ☐
4. Dry leaves go in the recycle bin. ☐
5. Clothes go in the compost bin. ☐
6. Iron nails go in the e-waste bin. ☐
7. Mobile phones go in the e-waste bin. ☐
8. Waste food goes in the recycle bin. ☐
9. Use-and-throw face masks go in the recycling bin. ☐
10. Nutshells go in the recycle bin. ☐
11. Batteries go in the compost bin. ☐
12. Glass goes in the e-waste bin. ☐
13. Newspapers go in the recycle bin. ☐
14. Vegetable stalks and skins go in the compost bin. ☐
15. Old shoes go in the e-waste bin. ☐
16. Waste food goes in the compost bin. ☐

World Around Us

25 Land of the Rising Sun

The Chinese were the first to mention Japan in one of their texts. To people in China, the Sun rose from the direction where Japan was located. So, they called the country the land of the rising sun.

Match Column A with Column B *to find out some interesting facts about Japan.*

	Column A		Column B
1	Japan has more than	a	Tokyo
2	Japan's four main islands cover	b	Sumo
3	In Japanese, the country name is	c	Origami
4	The currency is called	d	Osaka
5	The unofficial national flower is	e	6850 islands
6	Japanese wrestling is called	f	Sushi
7	The Japanese art of paper-folding is called	g	97% of its total land
8	The capital is	h	Cherry blossom
9	The main port city in Japan is	i	Nippon or Nihon
10	A popular Japanese food is	j	Yen

Whiz fact

Kimono is the traditional Japanese dress. It consists of a long, full-sleeved robe wrapped around the body, with a sash called 'obi' tied around it.

Language and Literature

26 Roald Dahl

Roald Dahl is loved not only for his wonderful stories but also for the weird and wonderful characters he created.

Match the characters and brief plot in column A to the book in column B in which these characters appear.

Column A

1. Aunt Spiker and Aunt Sponge ill-treat their nephew who runs away in a fruit and ends up in New York.
2. A family of Muggle Wumps and the Roly-Poly Bird plot to punish a dreadful couple, and eventually escape after gluing the couple upside down to the floor.
3. Bruno Jenkins and his Norwegian grandmother decide to rid the world of bald, wig-wearing, square-footed, claw-fingered evil women who want to turn all the children of England into mice.
4. Farmers Boggis, Bunce and Bean are outsmarted by an animal who steals their chickens, ducks and turkeys and feeds a bunch of underground animals a banquet.
5. Little Ms. M Wormwood goes to a school whose principal is the horrid Miss Trunchbull. Thanks to Miss Honey, everything sorts itself out in the end.
6. Little Sophie befriends a friendly giant, goes to Dream Country to catch and store dreams, visits Buckingham Palace, and eventually captures maneating giants and sets things right.
7. Five children get a golden ticket to visit Willy Wonka's factory, where the Oompa Loompas make the world's best chocolate.
8. When Mr and Mrs Kranky go out grocery shopping, their son feeds his grandmother a concoction of weird ingredients that makes her grow enormous.

Column B

a *Matilda*

b *Fantastic Mr. Fox*

c *The Twits*

d *Charlie and the Chocolate Factory*

e *The Witches*

f *James and the Giant Peach*

g *George's Marvellous Medicine*

h *The BFG*

Whiz fact

Many of Dahl's characters were based on people he'd met in real life. The grandmother in *The Witches* is based on his own grandmother and the little girl in *The BFG* was named after his granddaughter, Sophie.

India Focus

27 Northeast India

Northeast India has an interesting geography. Look at the map and write whether the sentences given below are true or false.

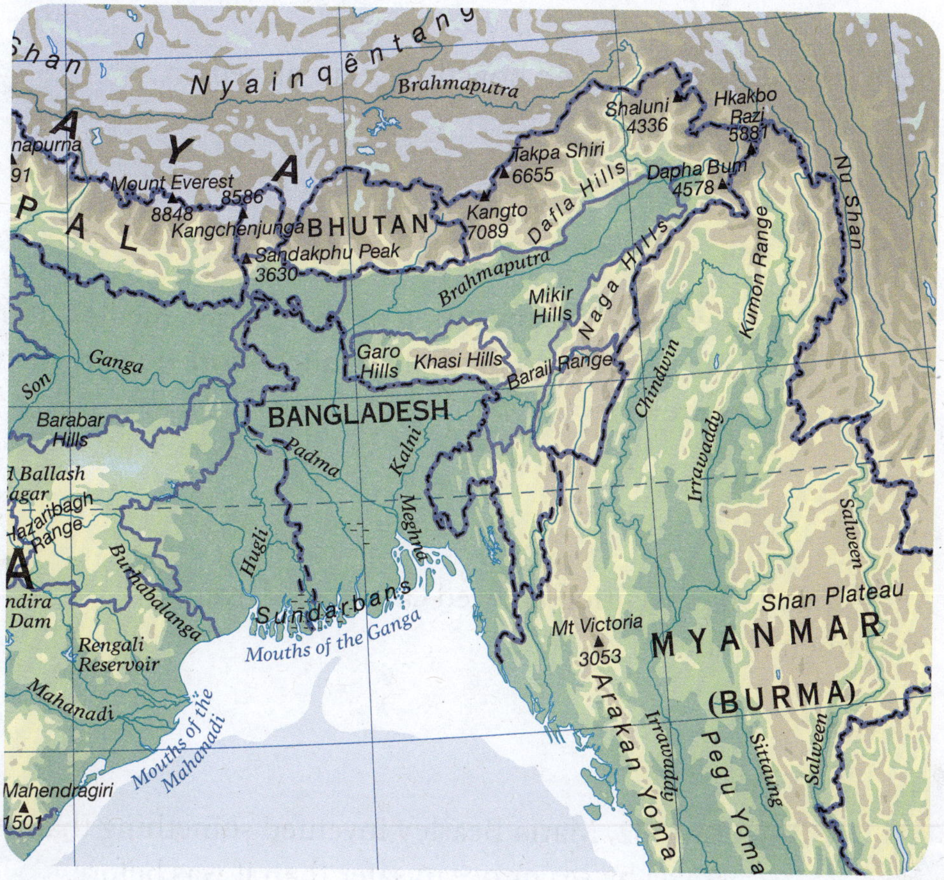

1. Khasi and Garo are names of rivers that flow through Meghalaya. ....
2. The Kangchenjunga peak bordering Sikkim and Nepal is more than 8000 metres tall. ....
3. The Brahmaputra flows through Assam and then into Bangladesh. ....
4. The Irawaddy is a river in Northeast India. ....
5. Kangto, Takpa Shiri and Shaluni are tall mountain peaks on the border between Arunachal Pradesh and China. ....
6. Sikkim is like a little finger between Nepal and Bhutan. ....
7. The Naga Hills are actually located in Myanmar. ....
8. The Ganga and the Son are two rivers in Northeast India. ....

28 Incredible Inventions by Women

Identify these inventions by women and fill in the blanks. Their names are given in the help box below.

1 Ellen Fitz helped us to understand how things are placed on Earth with her invention in 1875. ....

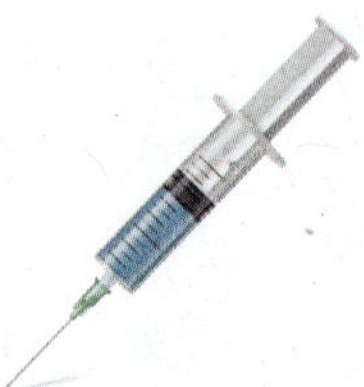

2 Letitia Geer's invention of 1899 allows medicine to reach our bodies and take effect much more quickly than if we were to swallow it. ....

3 Mary Anderson's 1903 invention allowed cars to be driven safely even when it rained. ....

4 In 1882, Maria Beasley invented something that would make travel by sea or ocean safer than it was before.

....

5 In 1845, Sarah Mather invented a device that made it easy for underwater vessels to view the surface of the water while staying hidden in the depths...

6 Margaret A. Wilcox created a system which directed air from over a car engine to warm the interiors.

....

7 In 1887, Anna Connelly invented a special kind of emergency exit to make buildings safe.

....

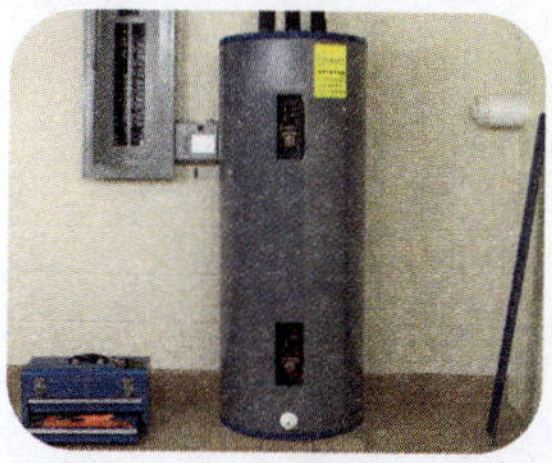

8 In 1917, Ida Forbes invented a machine which made hot water available much more easily than it was earlier.

....

9 In the 1960s, Marie van Brittan Brown set up a system by which a person inside a house could see the door and other external areas without having to actually open the door, thereby helping people ensure their own safety, without or before the arrival of the police.

....

10 Indian-origin Singapore resident Pranoti Nagarkar-Israni's invention helps any homemaker or chef literally churn out flatbreads at the pace of one a minute. What's more, it is equipped with machine learning technology, so it adapts, corrects and improves itself on the go!

....

Help box

Globe | Medical syringe | Life raft | Electric water heater | Home security system | Roti maker | Car heater | Windshield wiper | Submarine telescope | Fire escape

Whiz fact

In the early years of the United States, women inventors were not granted patents. When Sybilla Masters developed a new corn mill, she was denied a patent and three years later, her husband was granted the patent for her invention.

India Focus

29 Jaipur

Jaipur is the state capital of Rajasthan and its largest city. It is a UNESCO World Heritage Site.

Complete this brief essay about Jaipur with names from the help box.

1. Jaipur was founded in 1727 by .... He also set up the famed ...., which houses one of the five astronomical observatories in India, and also has the Samrat Yantra, which is the world's biggest sundial. .... Fort, a fort near Jaipur is a UNESCO World Heritage site.

2. An iconic monument of Jaipur is the five-storeyed ...., or Palace of Winds, which was built so that women of the royal family could watch processions in the city through the .... or latticed windows.

3. Maharani ...., who married Sawai Man Singh II of the princely state of Jaipur in 1940, fought for the upliftment of women and, among other things, revived some of the ancient ceramic craft traditions, including .... of Jaipur, which now has a GI tag.

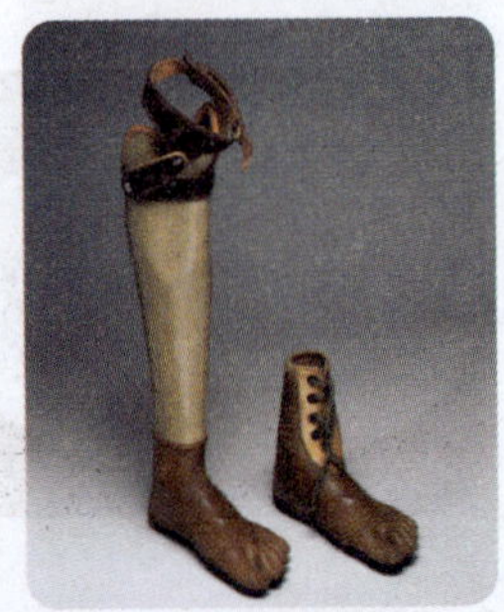

4. In 1968, Ram Chandra Sharma designed a prosthetic limb called the ...., used widely by people who need an artificial limb.

5. The modern city of Jaipur is an export hub for jewellery, textiles, furniture and handicrafts, and also attracts thousands of visitors for events such as the Jaipur ...., the largest literary festival in the world.

Help box

Gayatri Devi | Sawai Jai Singh II | Hawa Mahal | Jaipur foot | Lit Fest | Amer | Jantar Mantar | blue pottery | *jaalis*

Whiz fact

In 1876, Jaipur was painted pink to welcome the Prince of Wales and since then, because of its distinctive appearance, it has come to be known as the Pink City.

Life on Land

30 Upcycle

Taking an old thing and improving, repurposing, upgrading and beautifying it so that it is reused without that 'hand-me-down' feel is called upcycling.

Look at these pictures and the descriptions and match the original items with their upcycled versions.

Original Item	Description	Upcycled Item
1 	Your vertical garden grows out of a soil-filled transparent horizontal 'pot'.	a 
2 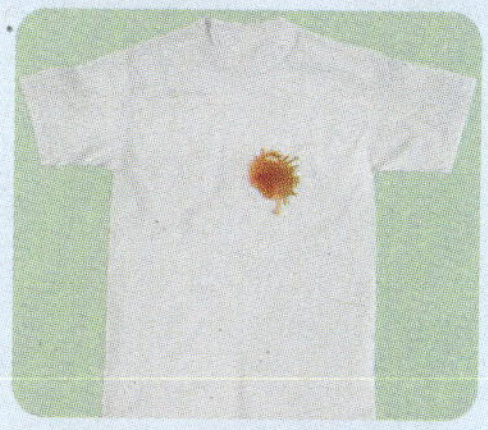	The stain marks are given a design using colourful sequins.	b 
3 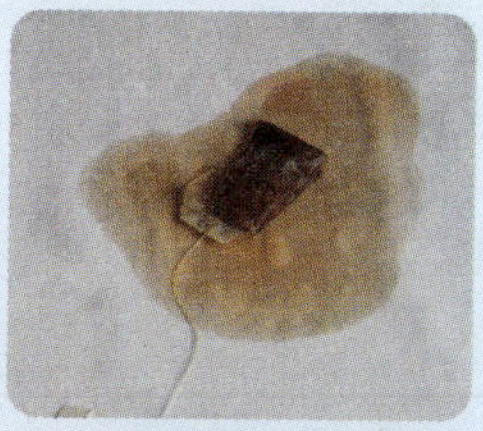	Tea water stain gives a lovely sepia colour.	c 
4 	Carry bags can be made up of old cotton clothes.	d 
5 	Plants are not fussy about pots of a particular shape, they're not too big for their boots.	e 
6 	Origami is a great way to fold paper into fun shapes.	f 

Life Skills

37 PIN Codes

PROBLEM SOLVING

The 6-digit number at the end of an address is the Postal Index Number or PIN code. Giving the PIN code helps the postman deliver the letter or package to the correct address. For example, the PIN code 411001 can be understood in this way:

4	1	1	0	0	1
The first digit stands for one of India's nine postal zones.	The second digit indicates the sub-zone. It is normally read with the first digit.	The third digit indicates the sorting district within the sub-zone.	The last three digits are assigned to individual post offices.		
4 stands for Maharashtra, Goa, Madhya Pradesh and Chhattisgarh.	**1** will be read with the first digit to make 41, the sub-region in which Pune falls.	**1** is Sorting District 1 in Pune.	**001** stands for the Pune General Post Office or GPO.		

Look at the map that has the first two digits of the PIN code of each state. Use the help box to find the PIN codes of the GPOs in various cities.

1. Ahmedabad ....
2. Chennai ....
3. Bhubaneswar ....
4. Shimla ....
5. Jaipur ....
6. Itanagar ....
7. Gangtok ....
8. Lucknow ....
9. Bengaluru ....
10. Port Blair ....

Help box

171001	226001	380001	302001	560002
600001	737101	744101	751001	791111

Whiz fact

The ninth postal zone, that is, PIN codes beginning with the number 9 are for Army Post Offices and Field Post Offices.

General Science

32 Indian Scientists

These Indian scientists achieved global recognition for their achievements.

Read the statements given below and use the help box to write the names of the Indian Scientists who were globally recognised for their work.

1. Considered the Father of the Indian Space Programme, ... set up the Indian Space Research Organisation (ISRO) and other reputed institutions such as the Indian Institute of Management, Ahmedabad (IIM-A).

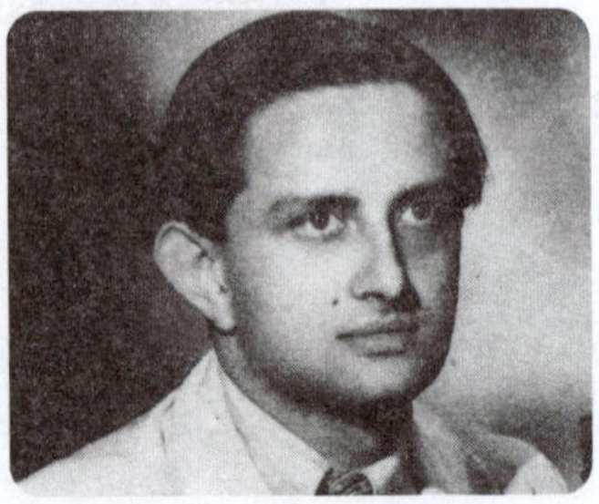

2. .... won the Nobel Prize for Physics in 1930 for his work on the scattering of light. He was the first Asian to win a Nobel Prize in the sciences.

3. .... was an Indian-American biochemist who shared the Nobel Prize for Physiology or Medicine in 1968 with Marshall Nirenberg and Robert Holley for showing how the order of nucleotides controls the cell's synthesis of proteins.

4. .... is known as the father of Indian nuclear power. He was against manufacturing atomic bombs, preferring instead to use nuclear power to reduce poverty and increase the well-being of people.

5 .... was an ornithologist and naturalist called the 'Birdman of India'. He was among the first Indians to conduct systematic bird surveys across the country.

6 .... pioneered the study of radio and microwave optics and first demonstrated wireless communication. He also invented the crescograph to measure plant response to various actions, showing that plants can feel pain and understand affection.

7 .... formulated the Saha Equation, which is one of the basic tools in astrophysics. He is also the chief architect of river planning in India and prepared the original plan of the Damodar Valley Project.

8 .... was an Indian physicist who specialised in quantum mechanics. He collaborated with Albert Einstein and also has a class of subatomic particles named after him.

Help box

CV Raman | Meghnad Saha | Satyendra Nath Bose | Homi Bhabha | Salim Ali | Vikram Sarabhai | Har Gobind Khorana | Jagadish Chandra Bose

Whiz fact

Srinivasa Ramanujan was a mathematician who made remarkable contributions to mathematical analysis, number theory, infinite series and continued fractions. He has been immortalised in many ways including a book and a film called *The Man Who Knew Infinity*.

Climate Action

33 Global Warming

Global warming is the slow increase in the overall temperature of the Earth's atmosphere due to the greenhouse effect.

Fill in the blanks with the words given in the help box to find out ten things you can do to reduce global warming. Words from the help box may be used more than once.

1 Plant more .... They absorb carbon dioxide and give out oxygen, reducing the amount of .... in the air.

2 Use less fuel. Reducing the use of fuels which release .... gases will help reduce pollution in the atmosphere.

3 Use wind and solar .... to power homes and devices. These do not release greenhouse ....

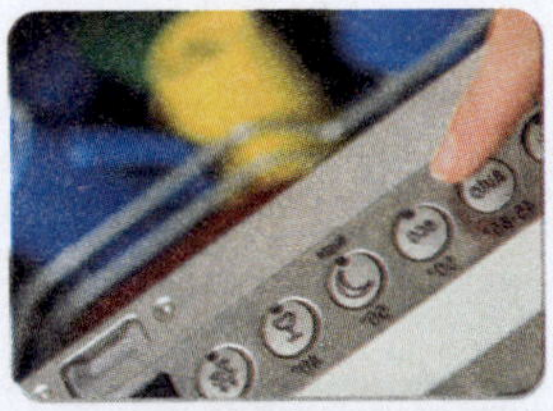

4 Use energy-efficient appliances. The less .... your appliances need, the less fuel they will use.

5 Make sure the doors and windows of your house close tightly to prevent cool air or warm air from escaping. This will prevent wastage of cooling and ....

6 Use less water. Transporting clean water to your home consumes energy, so the less .... you use, the more .... you save.

7 Buy energy-efficient .... These give light using very little energy and they last long too.

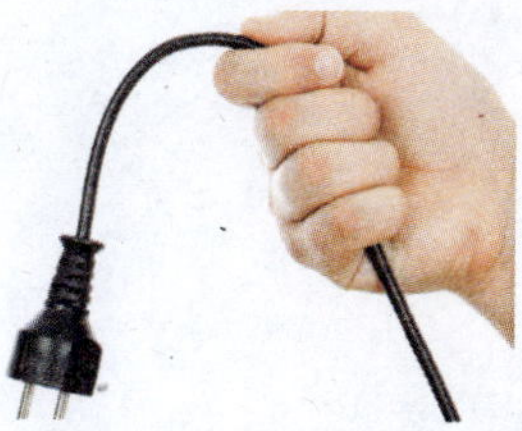

8 Unplug devices and appliances when not in use. Even if the switch is off, the plug will still consume some power if it is in the ....

9 Use .... transport. It uses less fuel and causes less pollution.

10 Tell others about global .... and encourage them to follow the steps detailed above.

Help box

greenhouse | energy | heating | water | bulbs | trees | socket | public | carbon dioxide | gases | warming

Whiz fact

The Arctic is melting so rapidly that scientists are expecting it to have a completely ice-free summer by 2040 or even earlier.

Natural World

34 Volcanoes

Volcanoes are living proof that the Earth was once too hot for life to exist. It is only when the earth's crust cooled enough that plant and later animal life began.

Given below is a world map with some prominent volcanoes marked on it. Using the facts given below, write the correct number in the box provided on the map alongside its location.

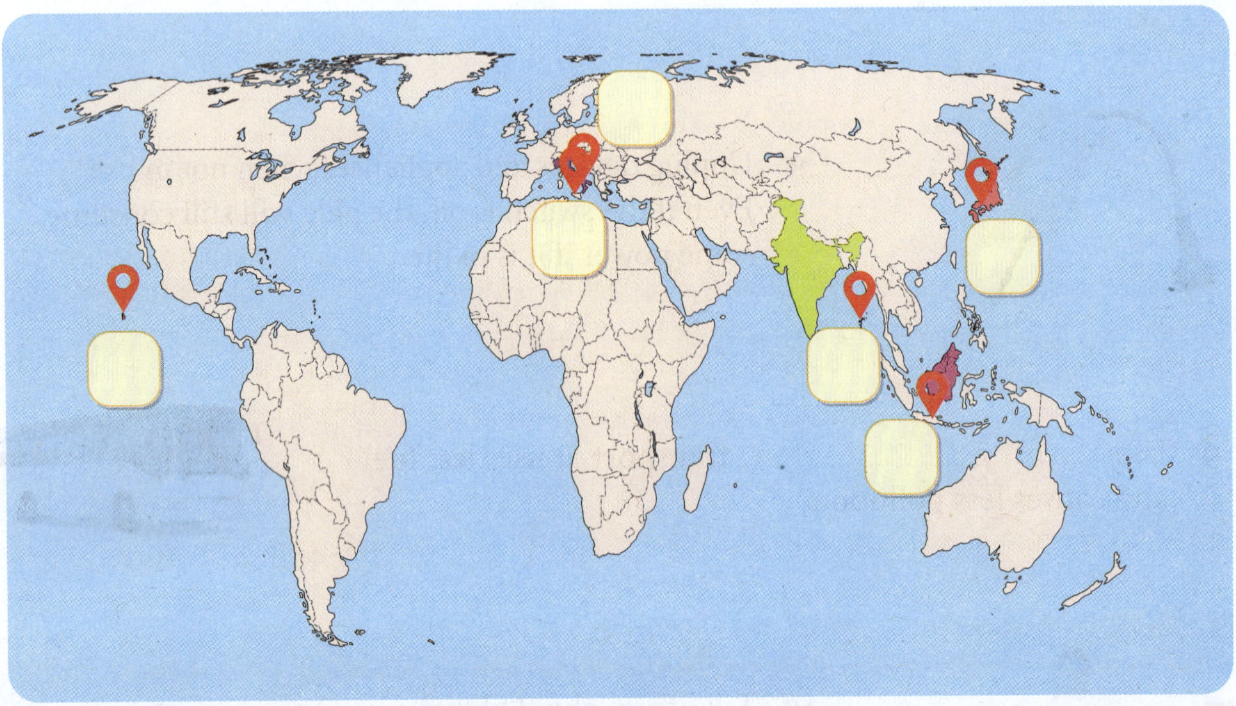

1 The Indonesian volcano Krakatoa's eruption in 1883 was 10,000 times more powerful than the atomic bomb dropped in Hiroshima. It erupted in 1928 and created a small island named Anak Krakatau or 'Child of Krakatoa'.

2 Mount Etna is the highest volcano in Europe. It is located on the island of Sicily in Italy.

3 Mauna Loa, the largest volcano in the world, is located in Hawaii. Its name means 'long mountain' in Hawaiian. It last erupted in 1984.

4 Mount Fuji is the highest mountain peak of Japan. It last erupted in 1707, but is still considered active by geologists.

5 India's only active volcano is the Barren Island volcano located in the Andaman and Nicobar Islands. Its 1991 eruption destroyed several animal and bird species.

6 Mount Vesuvius in Southern Italy is the only active volcano in mainland Europe. Its eruption in 79 CE destroyed Pompeii and Herculaneum, two prominent cities of the Roman Empire.

Whiz quiz

Find out the names of these volcanoes that have caused the most destruction in the world.

1 ...., Indonesia

2 ...., Martinique

3 ...., Colombia

4 ...., Japan

Whiz fact

The first time an active volcano was found other than on Earth was when NASA's Voyager 1 identified active volcanoes on Io, a moon of Jupiter, in 1979. Since then, active volcanoes have been identified on Jupiter, Saturn and Neptune as well.

35 Indian Paintings

India has a rich tradition of painting and many styles have developed in different regions. *Find out the names of some of these painting traditions by solving the riddles.*

1. My first is in MAKE, but not in CAKE ....
My second is in PANT, but not in PINT ....
My third is in DAMP, but not in CAMP ....
My fourth is in HUT, but not in CUT ....
My fifth is in BUT, but not in BAT ....
My sixth is in BILL, but not in HILL ....
My seventh is in FAR, but not in FUR ....
My eighth is in NEAT, but not in FEAT ....
My ninth is in PINK, but not in PUNK ....
.... is a centuries-old style of painting from Mithila in Bihar that gets its name from the words for honey and forest.

2. My first is in LAME, but not in LAKE ....
My second is in MAIL, but not in MAUL ....
My third is in TEEN, but not in TEEM ....
My fourth is in JIG, but not in JAG ....
My fifth is in SLAM, but not in SLIM ....
My sixth is in CART, but not in CARD ....
My seventh is in FULL, but not in FELL ....
My eighth is in DIRT, but not in DINT ....
My ninth is in SALE, but not in SALT ....
The Mughal Emperors, especially Akbar, Jahangir and Shah Jahan, popularised these tiny, highly detailed paintings, called .... paintings, that were usually a part of books.

3 My first is in WAR, but not in CAR ....

My second is in MANE, but not in MINE ....

My third is in DARK, but not in DANK ....

My fourth is in LOW, but not in COW ....

My fifth is in BIT, but not in BUT ....

.... art, created with white paste made from rice and water, is named after the group of tribal people who make these paintings.

4 My first is in PICK, but not in TICK ....

My second is in GOAT, but not in GOUT ....

My third is in PATH, but not in PATE ....

My fourth is in SACK, but not in SICK ....

My fifth is in RIM, but not in DIM ....

My sixth is in SING, but not in SANG ....

The .... style of painting, its name comes from the Hindi word for mountain, was largely based in the historic district of Kangra in Himachal Pradesh.

5 My first is in TAIL, but not in PAIL ....

My second is in GAVE, but not in GIVE ....

My third is in BONE, but not in BORE ....

My fourth is in JOWL, but not in HOWL ....

My fifth is in BOAT, but not in BEAT ....

My sixth is in CART, but not in CAST ....

My seventh is in FARE, but not in FARM ....

.... paintings, which are known for their use of gold paint and semi-precious stones, are named after a town in Tamil Nadu, which is also called Thanjavur.

Whiz fact

The earliest Indian paintings were rock paintings of pre-historic times, which can be seen in caves at Bhimbetka in Madhya Pradesh. Some of these paintings are as old as 30,000 years!

Sports

36 Great Sportspeople

The names of some great sportspersons and their achievements are listed below.

Fill in the blanks with the sports that they played.

1. Sir Don Bradman was an Australian with a batting average of 99.94 in test matches, the highest ever.

C.......... .... C.......... ....T

2. Tiger Woods is a US sensation, the youngest to achieve the career Grand Slam in his sport.

.... OL ....

3. Muhammad Ali was the world heavyweight champion three times.

B .... I .... G

4. Michael Phelps won 28 Olympic medals including 23 golds, more than any other sportsperson ever.

S .... MM .... G

5. Nadia Comaneci, a Romanian woman, was the first to record a score of perfect ten in her sport at the Olympics.

G .... AS .... C ....

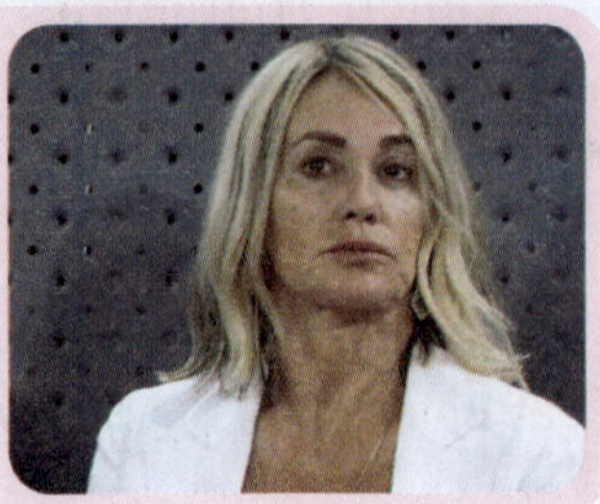

6 Michael Jordan is the greatest player of all time in this sport according to the National Association of this sport in the USA.

B .... K .... B L

7 Pele, the Brazilian player is considered on the greatest players of all time in this sport.

.... OO .... B L

8 Jesse Owens is the US athlete who won four gold medals at the 1936 Olympics, and broke three world records in 1935.

A .... L .... T .... C ....

9 Dhyan Chand was an Indian Army officer known as the Wizard. He was part of three Olympic gold-winning teams.

.... OC .... Y

10 Martina Navratilova is the Czech-American woman star who won 167 singles titles, the most ever by one player.

T .... N .... S

Whiz fact

Vishwanathan Anand became India's first chess grandmaster in 1988. He held the FIDE World Chess Championship from 2000 to 2002, became the undisputed World Champion in 2007 and defended his title in 2008, 2010 and 2012. In 2007, he received the Padma Vibhushan.

Natural World

37 Animal Kingdom

We have all seen different animals. Let's take two examples: crows and cockroaches. Both have wings, both can fly, and both are seen around houses. But what makes a crow a bird and a cockroach an insect? What are the differences between them?

Here is a very short and simple list of animal features, movements, habitats and groups.

Animal features: bones, shell, eggs, babies, feathers, scales, hair, lungs, gills

Movements: fly, swim, crawl, walk, hop

Habitats: land, water

Animal groups: mammals, birds, fish, reptiles, amphibians, insects

Choose the correct answers from this list given above and fill in the blanks to get details about each of the animals in the sentences. One has been done for you.

1. A bat is a mammal. The bones in its body give it its shape and its body is covered with hair. Bats use their lungs to breathe. These creatures live on land and can fly to move from one place to another.

2. A crab has a .... that gives it shape and protects its body. Crabs .... sideways while moving and they breathe using their ....

3. An ostrich is a .... give it its shape. Although its body is covered in .... it cannot .... It breathes using its .... and lives on ....

4 Whales are amongst the largest creatures in the animal kingdom. Although they live in ...., they are .... They breathe using their .... and .... to move. .... give them their body shape. They have smooth skin with a little bit of .... on their bodies.

5 Frogs are .... that live on .... and .... They .... to move from one place to another on land and in water, they ....

6 Lizards are .... and their skin is covered in .... They live on .... and they breathe using their .... To move, lizards ....

7 A crocodile is part of the .... family and lives on .... and in .... Its body structure is formed by .... underneath a body covered with .... It breathes using .... and .... to move from one place to another on land.

8 A fish .... from place to place. .... give it its shape and .... cover its body. It breathes using ....

Whiz fact

Reptiles are cold-blooded. This means that the body temperature of these animals changes with that of their environments.

India Focus

38 Women Freedom Fighters

Many women contributed greatly to the Indian freedom struggle.

Fill in the blanks with the names of some prominent Indian women freedom fighters.

1. An English woman who fought for democracy in India, she became the President of the Indian National Congress. ....

2. She formed the Rani of Jhansi Regiment, the women's division of Subhash Chandra Bose's Indian National Army.
....
3. She walked and worked in-step with her famous husband in the fight for India's independence. ....
4. She left her comfortable life in London to join the Indian National Movement and was most remembered for her efforts to revive traditional handicrafts.
....
5. A fearless warrior and patriot, she fought against the British annexing her kingdom, Jhansi. ....
6. She revolted against the British and also fought against the destruction of temples and mosques in Oudh. ....

7. The poems of this 'Nightingale of India' inspired many Indians to stand up for their rights and fight British rule.
....
8. She was arrested for her participation in the Salt Satyagraha and led the Quit India Movement when she was released. ....

Help box

Rani Lakshmibai | Lakshmi Sahgal | Kasturba Gandhi | Begum Hazrat Mahal | Annie Besant | Aruna Asaf Ali | Sarojini Naidu | Kamaladevi Chattopadhyay

Whiz fact

Rani Gaidinliu of Manipur fought against the British and was arrested and imprisoned. She was acknowledged for her many sacrifices by Jawaharlal Nehru.

39 Aadhaar Card

An Aadhaar Card is a proof of identity.

Look at the front and reverse sides of this Aadhaar Card. Look at your Aadhaar card and tick the information you can see on it.

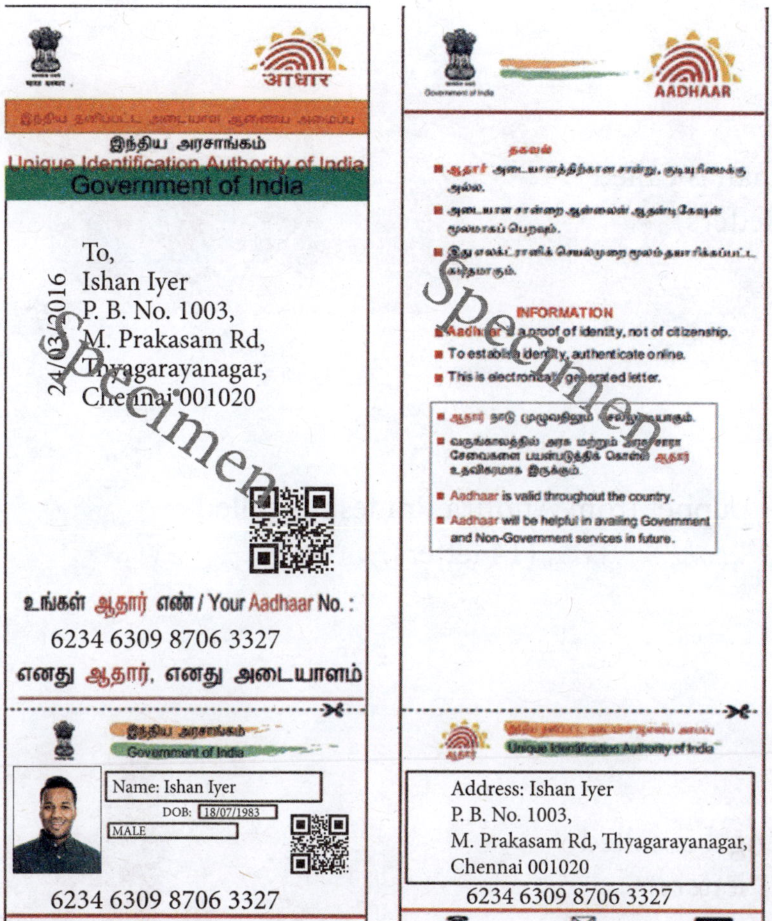

1. Name ☐
2. Age ☐
3. Gender ☐
4. Parent's name ☐
5. Photograph ☐
6. Phone number ☐
7. Emblem of India ☐
8. Date of birth ☐
9. Place of birth ☐
10. Nationality ☐
11. File no. ☐
12. Aadhaar no. ☐

Look at your Adhaar Card and answer these questions.

1. In which two languages is the information given?

   ....

2. What information is given at the back of the Aadhaar Card?

   ....

40 Puppets of India

Puppets are a popular form of entertainment for children as well as adults. There are many kinds of puppets—glove, string, rod, shadow and many more.

Use the clues and the help box to fill in the names of traditional puppets from different states of India.

1 The string puppet from Rajasthan is called .... (9 letters)

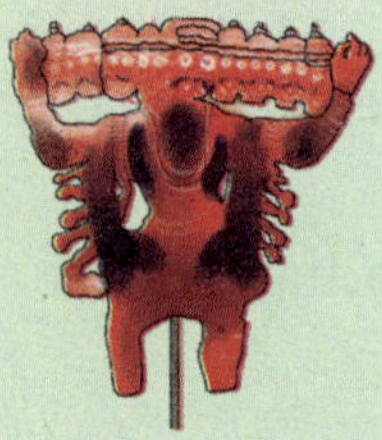

2 The shadow puppet from Andhra Pradesh is called .... (14 letters)

3 The rod puppet from West Bengal is called .... (11 letters)

4 The glove puppet from Odisha is called .... (16 letters)

5 The glove puppet from Kerala is called .... (10 letters)

6 The string puppet from Karnataka is called .... (10 letters)

7 The string puppet from Maharashtra is called .... (16 letters)

8 Made of light wood, the Odisha puppet has no legs but wears long flowing skirt. This string puppet is called .... (7 letters).

Help box

Pavakoothu	*Tholu Bommalata*	*Kundhei*	*Gombeyatta*
Kathputli	*Putul Nautch*	*Kathikundhei Nach*	*Kalasutri-bahulya*

Whiz fact

Tamil Nadu has a form of string puppet called *bommalattam*.

47 Celebrate Safely

Life Skills

We all enjoy celebrating festivals. There are so many different ways to celebrate them! But it is important that we celebrate safely so that we don't hurt ourselves or others.

Match the columns for what could happen for each unsafe behaviour listed below.

Unsafe behaviour

1 If you light oil lamps in a closed staircase,

2 If you light crackers on your hand,

3 If you eat too much heavy food during a festival,

4 If you wear fancy new clothes that sweep the ground on a festival day,

What could happen

a you could get lost in the crowd.

b the colour could go into their eyes and it can be painful.

c your clothes could get badly soiled from spilt food or oil.

d they could explode on you or another person and cause a lot of damage.

5 If you fling a handful of dry colour on someone's face,

6 If you get separated from your elders in a fair or place of worship,

7 If you hang Christmas tree ornaments when the tree lights are lit,

8 If you throw water balloons or water from a height,

9 If you use chemical instead of natural or organic colours,

e the flame of the lamps could spread and cause a big fire.

f you could have an upset stomach.

g the colour may not come off easily or it could cause allergies.

h you could get an electric shock from loose or hanging wires as you decorate.

i you could hurt or injure people badly, apart from getting them wet.

World Around Us

42 The Mighty Himalayas

Use the help box to find out some interesting facts about the Himalayas, the youngest mountain ranges in the world.

1 The Himalayas, which include several smaller mountain ranges, pass through India, Pakistan, ..., China, Bhutan and Nepal.

2 Geological tests confirm that this range is still rising by approximately .... per year.

3 The Himalayan range has approximately 15,000 glaciers. At 76 kilometres long, the .... Glacier is second longest in the world outside the polar region, only 1 kilometre smaller than the Fedchenko Glacier in Tajikistan.

4 The Himalayas are home to the third largest ice deposits in the world, after the Arctic and ....

5 Mount Everest, the highest peak on Earth, was named by ...., a British army officer, to honour Colonel George Everest, Surveyor General of India from 1830 to 1843.

6 Sir Edmund Hillary and Sherpa mountaineer .... were the first people to climb to the summit of Mount Everest, in 1953.

7 Himalayan peaks popular for climbing include the Everest, Kanchenjunga, Lhotse and ....

8 The Himalayas are often called the ....

Help box

Antarctica	Sir Andrew Waugh	roof of the world	2 cm
Dhaulagiri	Siachen	Tenzing Norgay	Afghanistan

Whiz fact

Mount Everest, the highest mountain peak in the Himalayas, has different names amongst the peoples who live around it. In Nepal, it is called *Sagarmatha*, meaning 'forehead in the sky'. The Tibetans call it *Chomolungma*, meaning 'Mother Goddess of the universe'.

India Focus

43 Gateway of India

Read these lines about the most visited tourist attraction of Mumbai. Using the words given in the help box, complete the story of the Gateway of India.

The Gateway of India is a monument located by the Arabian Sea at the southern tip of Mumbai, right opposite the iconic (1) .... It was built to commemorate the 1911 visit of (2) .... and (3) .... to Bombay, as the city was called then.

The Gateway was designed in Indo-Saracenic or Indo-Mughal style by the Scottish architect (4) .... It was built using yellow basalt and concrete and the construction was completed in 1924.

The Gateway is located on a pier called (5) ...., overlooking the Mumbai harbour. Boats from this pier ferry passengers to the (6) ...., famous for its cave temples.

In 1948, the last British soldiers marched out through the Gateway marking the end of the British Rule in India. The British who arrived by sea, ultimately left by sea and the Gateway of India became their port of departure.

Help box

Elephanta Island	Taj Mahal Palace	George Wittet
Apollo Bunder	Queen Mary	King George V

Whiz quiz

There are two statues situated near the Gateway of India. Look at the pictures and write whose statues they are.

(1) ....

(2) ....

World Around Us

44 Our Western Neighbour

Use the help box and fill in the blanks to find out some interesting facts about Pakistan.

1 The world's former No. 1 professional squash player, who holds the Guinness World Record for the longest winning streak by any athlete in top-level professional sports is ....

2 .... juice is the national drink of Pakistan.

3 Sialkot, a city in Pakistan, is the world's largest producer of handsewn ....

4 The national animal of Pakistan is the ....

5 The largest deep seaport in the world is ....

6 The world's highest polo ground in North Pakistan is in ....

7 The largest city of Pakistan is ....

8 The world's largest man-made forest, originally planted in 1866 by British foresters, is ....

9 The national flower of Pakistan is ....

10 The shape of the .... lake resembles a tear.

11 The capital of Pakistan is ....

12 The national bird of Pakistan ....

13 The .... is an endangered freshwater species found in the Indus River.

14 .... is the world's only fertile desert.

Help box

chukar partridge, Jahangir Khan, Changa Manga, footballs, Ansoo, jasmine, sugarcane, markhor, Gwadar Port, Tharparkar, Karachi, Islamabad, Shandur Pass, blind dolphin

Whiz fact

Urdu is the national language of Pakistan and English is its official language, but the most spoken language is Punjabi.

Science

45 India in Space

The Indian Space Research Organisation (ISRO) is the space agency of the Government of India. Its headquarters are in Bengaluru. Its vision is to 'harness space technology for national development while pursuing space science research and planetary exploration.'

Use the help box to complete the following sentences about India and Indians in space.

1. .... in Andhra Pradesh is a rocket launching site.

2. On 5 November 2013, the Indian Space Research Organisation (ISRO) launched ...., translatable as Mars Orbiter, thus becoming the first Asian country to orbit Mars and the first in the entire world to succeed on its first attempt.

3. The first woman of Indian origin in space who flew on space shuttle *Columbia* in 1997 as a mission specialist and primary robotic arm operator was ....

4. ISRO built India's first satellite, named .... after the famous mathematician. It was launched by the Soviet Union on 19 April 1975.

5. ISRO sent lunar orbiter .... into space on 22 October 2008.

6. The first Indian to travel to space, ..., was a test pilot in the Indian Air Force, who went as part of a joint mission between ISRO and the Soviet Intercosmos Space Programme.

Help box

Aryabhata | Chandrayaan-1 | Kalpana Chawla | Mangalyaan | Rakesh Sharma | Sriharikota

Whiz fact

The only new Indian currency note to not have a monument in its design is the ₹2000 note, which features the Mangalyaan space probe.

46 Leaders of the World

Match the leaders with their achievements by writing the correct number in the boxes.

1 

Martin Luther King, Jr.

3 

Simon Bolivar

5 

Emmeline Pankhurst

7 

Nelson Mandela

a Fought to abolish slavery in the Southern States

b Sought to modernise Ethiopia and brought it into the United Nations

c An activist and humanitarian known for advancing civil rights for African Americans

d A British suffragette who dedicated her life to the promotion of women's rights

e The anti-apartheid revolutionary of South Africa

f The guerrilla leader of the Cuban Revolution who addressed everyone as 'che' or 'brother'

g Dedicated her life to helping others, she completely transformed the quality of care in times of war

h Freed his own country as well as Bolivia, Colombia, Ecuador, Peru and Panama from the Spanish Empire

2 

Abraham Lincoln

4 

Haile Selassie I

6 

Ernesto Guevara

8 

Florence Nightingale

Whiz fact

Mustafa Kemal Pasha abolished the Ottoman Empire and founded the Turkish republic in its place. He was granted the surname Atatürk which means 'Father of the Turks'.

Focus

47 Indian Armed Forces

The Indian Armed Forces consists primarily of three professional services—the Indian Army, the Indian Navy and the Indian Air Force. Each service has its own rank structure.

Fill in the blanks in the columns using the help box.

Indian Army	Indian Navy	Indian Air Force
1	Admiral of the Fleet	Marshal of the Air Force
General	2	Air Chief Marshal
Lieutenant General	Vice Admiral	3 ....
Major General	4	Air Vice Marshal
5	Commodore	Air Commodore
6	Captain	Group Captain
Lieutenant Colonel	Commander	7 ....
Major	Lieutenant Commander	8 ....
9	Lieutenant	Flight Lieutenant
Lieutenant	10	Flying Officer

Help box

Rear Admiral | Colonel | Air Marshal | Sub-Lieutenant | Wing Commander
Admiral | Field Marshal | Captain | Brigadier | Squadron Leader

World Around Us

48 Peoples Across Countries

Some countries are very new, and some countries are still ideas—they don't exist at this moment. Some people and communities live across many countries. Others are fighting for their own country. And yet others have never had a country; they are simply where they have been for centuries, and country borders have grown around them.

Read the descriptions of these people and use the help box and the extra clue and fill in the name.

Description	Clue	Name of community
1 A group of Middle Eastern people, their homeland is divided across Turkey, Iran, Iraq and Syria.	a The name rhymes with a synonym for yoghurt.	 i ....
2 Also known as Gypsies, these people of Indian origin are spread across Europe and the rest of the world.	b Despite their name, they do not come from the capital of Italy.	 ii ....
3 A group of people who became stateless in Myanmar because their language was deemed to be a dialect of Bengali, they are not considered native to Myanmar.	c They are sometimes called Rohang, or inhabitants of Arakan, the old name for Rakhine State, from where they traditionally hail.	 iii ....
4 A Turkic group of people who dominated the trade routes that crossed Central Asia, they now live in Xinjiang, China.	d The name sounds like a combination of "we" and the Hindi word for jaggery.	 iv ....

5 Followers of Buddhism, they consider the Dalai Lama their leader. Their mountainous homeland was occupied by China in 1950.

6 Sometimes also called Eskimos, these people live near the Arctic Circle across Alaska, Canada and Greenland.

7 A group of people with a distinct language, they live in Northeastern Spain and Southwestern France.

8 A nomadic people who travelled across the Sahara Desert, they found themselves divided across various countries after various countries were formed from French West Africa.

e Many of them live around Dharamshala in Himachal Pradesh. Their home is called "the roof of the world".

f Add a first-person pronoun with the French word for "night".

g Sounds like a verb that means "sitting or lying idly in the sun", rather like a crocodile.

h The origin of their name remains ambiguous, but sounds like a combination of the number 2, the letter "R" and an egg.

v ....

vi ....

vii ....

viii ....

Help box

Tibetans, Uyghur, Tuareg, Romani, Basque, Inuit, Kurds, Rohingya

Literacy Skills

49 Robotics

An exciting career for science aficionados is robotics.

Read this introduction to robotics and fill in the blanks using words from the help box. But watch out: there are some extra incorrect words!

TECHNOLOGY

1 Robotics involves the design, construction, operation, and use of robots. The goal of robotics as a discipline is to design machines—called robots—that can help .... do tasks.

2 Whilst a robot could be designed to look like a human, most are extremely .... in appearance.

3 Robots can replace humans in performing repetitive and dangerous tasks which humans prefer not to do, or are unable to do because of size limitations, or which take place in extreme .... such as outer space or the bottom of the sea.

4 Some robots do jobs that are dangerous to humans like defusing bombs or finding .... in buildings that may have collapsed.

5 The word 'robot' comes from Slavic languages and was first used to denote a fictional humanoid in a 1920 .... play by Karel Capek.

6 The first modern digital robot was invented by George Devol in 1954, who started Unimation, a robotics company. The first .... robot was sold to General Motors who used it in their automobile manufacturing factory.

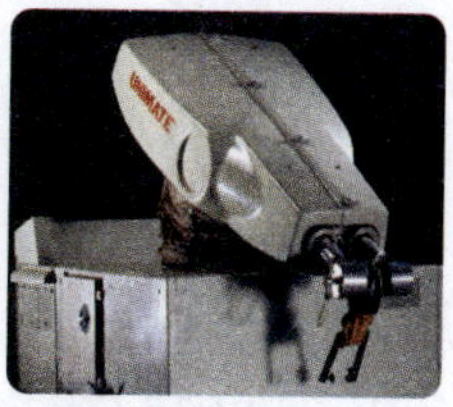

7 The word robot can refer to physical robots as well as virtual ones. Virtual ones are sometimes called ...., which are used in all kinds of softwares and virtual platforms. Some even 'chat' with users!

CHAT BOT

8 The word **robotics** was coined by the science fiction writer .... who also laid down the famous 3 Laws of Robotics:

- A robot may not injure a human nor allow a human to be harmed.
- A robot must obey humans except if the order might cause it to break the first law.
- A robot must protect itself unless it conflicts with the first or second law.

Help box

Isaac Asimov | functional | survivors | unimate | Sony | Czech | environments | aliens | bots | humans | french | realistic

Whiz fact

The Renaissance artist and sculptor Leonardo da Vinci sketched plans for a humanoid robot around 1495.

Quiz Yourself 1

Choose the correct answer from the given options.

1. What is the name of the intrepid sailor in the comic Tintin?
   (a) Müller (b) First Mate Alan
   (c) Captain Haddock (d) Rastapoupolos

2. This Venezuelan freed his country as well as Bolivia, Colombia, Ecuador, Peru and Panama from the Spanish Empire. What is his name?
   (a) Che Guevara (b) Simon Bolivar
   (c) Fidel Castro (d) Pablo Escobar

3. To which country does Agatha Christie's detective Hercule Poirot belong?
   (a) Greece (b) Switzerland (c) France (d) Belgium

4. Saputara is the only hill station of which state?
   (a) Rajasthan (b) Gujarat (c) Madhya Pradesh (d) Chhattisgarh

5. Global warming happens because of the presence of what kind of gases in the Earth's atmosphere?
   (a) Greenhouse (b) Hothouse (c) Natural (d) Toxic

6. Who fought to abolish slavery in the Southern States?
   (a) Ernesto Guevara (b) Nelson Mandela
   (c) Simon Bolivar (d) Abraham Lincoln

7. What is the Japanese art of paper-folding known as?
   (a) Ikebana (b) Origami (c) Kirigami (d) Bonsai

8. Bisi bele bath is a traditional food of which state?
   (a) Andhra Pradesh (b) Karnataka
   (c) Goa (d) Kerala

9. Along with Tenzing Norgay, who summited the highest peak in the world in 1953?
   (a) George Everest (b) Bachendri Pal
   (c) Edmund Hillary (d) Reinhard Messner

10. Which animals live in water but come up to the surface and breathe air through a blow hole?
    (a) Dolphins (b) Sharks (c) Seals (d) Octopuses

Quiz Yourself 2

Choose the correct answer from the given options.

1 Which city was the capital of India until 1911?

(a) Delhi (b) Mumbai (c) Kolkata (d) Agra

2 Which book by Roald Dahl features Miss Trunchbull and Miss Honey?

(a) Matilda (b) The Twits
(c) The BFG (d) Charlie and the Chocolate Factory

3 In which sport did Michael Phelps win 28 Olympic medals, more than any sportsperson ever?

(a) Athletics (b) Swimming
(c) Gymnastics (d) Tennis

4 What is the national language of Pakistan?

(a) Hindi (b) English (d) Urdu (b) Punjabi

5 Who was the first Indian to travel to space?

(a) Rakesh Sharma (b) Ravish Malhotra
(c) Sunita Williams (d) Kalpana Chawla

6 Which 1903 invention by Mary Anderson allowed cars to be driven safely even when it rained?

(a) Windshield (b) High beam
(c) Wipers (d) Rearview mirror

7 What is the national flower of Pakistan?

(a) Jasmine (b) Gulmohar (c) Rose (d) Champa

8 The flag of which country features five red crosses?

(a) Azerbaijan (b) Georgia (c) Switzerland (d) Turkey

9 The stylised peacock is part of the logo of which airline of one of India's neighbouring countries?

(a) Bangladesh (b) Bhutan (c) Sri Lanka (d) Pakistan

10 The flag of which Indian neighbouring country features a dragon?

(a) Sri Lanka (b) Nepal (c) Myanmar (d) Bhutan

Quiz Yourself 3

Choose the correct answer from the given options.

1 What did Jagadish Chandra Bose invent to measure plant response to various stimuli, showing that plants can feel pain and understand affection?

(a) Crescograph (b) Microscope (c) Mimeograph (d) Prism

2 Who formed the Rani of Jhansi Regiment, the women's division of Subhash Chandra Bose's Indian National Army and violently resisted the British?

(a) Annie Besant (b) Bhikaiji Cama
(c) Aruna Asaf Ali (d) Lakshmi Sahgal

3 Who is regarded as the father of India's space programme?

(a) Homi Bhabha (b) Abdul Kalam
(c) Vikram Sarabhai (d) CV Raman

4 What is the world's lowest point of land?

(a) Indira Point (b) Death Valley (c) Mauna Kea (d) Dead Sea

5 What is a group of frogs called?

(a) An army (b) A croak (c) A bunch (d) A bevy

6 In which script is Russian written?

(a) Roman (b) Aramaic (c) Greek (d) Cyrillic

7 Which of these Indian birds is on the critically endangered list?

(a) White Peacock (b) Vulture (c) Hawk (d) Crane

8 What is the head of the Indian Navy called?

(a) Admiral of the Fleet (b) Midshipman
(c) Captain (d) Commander

9 Which natural disaster occurs in the ocean and is characterised by strong winds, in the centre of which is a calm region called the eye?

(a) Tornado (b) Whirlpool (c) Cyclone (d) Tempest

10 Which folk painting form, created with white paste made from rice and water, is named after a tribe in Maharashtra?

(a) Kangra (b) Warli (c) Madhubani (d) Gond

Quiz Yourself 4

Choose the correct answer from the given options.

1 To which state does the string puppet called Kathputli belong?
(a) Rajasthan (b) Punjab
(c) Haryana (d) Uttar Pradesh

2 Which US athlete won four gold medals at the 1936 Olympics?
(a) Florence Griffiths-Joyner (b) Usain Bolt
(c) Ben Johnson (d) Jesse Owens

3 In which sport would you call the racquet a bat or a paddle?
(a) Table tennis (b) Rowing (c) Lacrosse (d) Squash

4 Which of these examples of waste should be disposed of in the compost bin?
(a) Bulbs (b) Fruit peels (c) Clothes (d) Wires

5 Which British woman led the Suffragette Movement that fought for women's rights?
(a) Marie Curie (b) Rosa Parks
(c) Emmeline Pankhurst (d) Margaret Thatcher

6 Name the community that are followers of Buddhism and consider Dalai Lama as their leader.
(a) Uyghur (b) Tibetans (c) Tuareg (d) Rohingya

7 Which specialist doctor treats the diseases of the heart?
(a) Cardiologist (b) Oncologist
(c) Paediatrician (d) Neonatologist

8 What does a crocodile use to breathe?
(a) Gills (b) Skin (c) Lungs (d) Blowhole

9 Which small, fluffy breed of dog got its name from an area located in Northern Poland and Germany along the Baltic Sea?
(a) Pomeranian (b) Alsatian (c) Chihuahua (d) Dalmatian

10 If a pincode begins with the number 9, which postal zone does it come under?
(a) Border (b) Army
(c) Union Territories (d) National Capital

Answer Key

Page 9: **Across:** 1. Snoopy; 3. Popeye; 5. Archie; 7. Dennis; 8. Dora; 9. Mickey

Down: 1. Superman; 2. Wonder Woman; 4. Garfield; 6. Haddock

Page 10: 1. Swahili; 2. Marhba; 3. goodbye; 6. Salut; 5. thank you

Page 11: 1. Tomorrow; 2. Assassination; 3. Independent; 4. Necessary; 5. Mischievous; 6. Conscious; 7. Hygiene; 8. Calendar; 9. Definite; 10. Absence

Page 12-13: **Across:** 3. Siberian Husky; 4. German Shepherd; 6. Scottish Terrier; 7. Pomeranian; 8. Chihuahua

Down: 1. Irish Setter; 2. English Foxhound; 5. French Bulldog

Page 14: 1. roundabout ahead; 2. pedestrian crossing prohibited; 3. school ahead; 4. falling rocks; 5. slippery road ahead; 6. speed breaker; 7. steep descent; 8. right hair pin bend; 9. no U-turn; 10. dangerous dip ahead; 11. speed limit 50 km per hour; 12. one-way street

Page 15: a. safe; b. easily; c. medicines; d. tools; e. January; f. watching; g. variants; h. letters; i. alphabet; j. understand

Page 16: 1. fever; 2. leap; 3. tower; 4. caravan; 5. knot; 6. army; 7. crash; 8. band; 9. pack

Page 17: 1. T; 2. O; 3. T; 4. O; 5. T; 6. O

Page18-19: 1. b. iii; 2. d. ii; 3. e. i; 4. a. v; 5. c. iv; 6. h. vii; 7. f. xi; 8. i. x; 9. j. ix; 10. k. viii; 11. g. vi

Page 20-21: 1. e; 2. a; 3. b; 4. c; 5. d; 6. g; 7. j; 8. i; 9. h; 10. f

Page 22-23: 1. Rouble; 2. Siberian tiger; 3. Trans-Siberian Railway; 4. Cyrillic; 5. Volga; 6. Baikal; 7. Taiga; 8. Tsar; 9. Kremlin; 10. Eurasian brown bear

Page 24: 1. b; 2. c; 3. f; 4. a; 5. e; 6. d

Page 25: **Across:** 4. Reindeer; 6. Starfish; 7. Octopus

Down: 1. Penguin; 2. Jellyfish; 3. Hippopotamus; 5. Dolphin; 6. Seal

Page 26-27: 1. Howrah Bridge, Hooghly; 2. Sundarbans; 3. Rabindranath Tagore; 4. Satyajit Ray; 5. Eden Gardens; 6. Kolkata; 7. Bay of Bengal; 8. Darjeeling; 9. hilsa, sandesh; 10. fishing cat

Page 28-29: 1.P, G; 2. Q, U; 3. M, R; 4. B, O; 5. N, C, A; 6. T, K; 7.Y, X; 8. E, W; 9. I, V; 10. D, Z; 11. S; 12.H, L

Page 30-31: 1. Hercule Poirot; 2. Jane Marple; 3. Arthur Hastings; 4. Ariadne Oliver; 5. *Orient Express;* 6. grey cells; 7. Parker Pyne; 8. Tommy, Tuppence; 9. Felicity Lemon; 10. Inspector Japp; 11. *Buckle, Shoe;* 12. Colonel Race

Page 32-33

P	U	A	W	N	I	R	E	K	I	D	A	M	D
M	P	A	V	G	Q	G	U	L	M	A	R	G	A
U	B	A	T	N	U	O	M	V	P	K	F	J	R
N	Z	R	U	V	R	V	G	A	E	F	G	S	J
N	Y	T	O	O	V	P	C	G	A	K	L	M	E
A	A	Y	E	U	E	H	I	S	T	L	A	N	E
R	D	I	Q	A	M	E	E	I	I	T	A	G	L
T	C	J	N	A	V	E	C	H	H	C	U	P	I
S	V	A	R	I	W	Q	I	E	Y	K	B	M	N
D	P	H	T	M	T	N	R	O	R	Q	Y	A	G
V	I	G	T	V	R	A	N	P	O	S	A	N	O
B	O	B	W	O	N	K	L	F	Z	W	T	A	Z
U	E	Q	M	E	G	H	U	P	O	A	G	L	J
J	A	S	A	P	U	T	A	R	A	Y	R	I	H

A. 12, Morni Hills; B. 6, Manali; C. 9, Saputara; D. 10, Munnar; E. 1, Ooty; F. 7, Nainital; G. 2, Mount Abu; H. 5, Pachmarhi; I. 3, Matheran; J. 8, Madikeri; K. 4, Darjeeling; L. 11, Gulmarg

Page 34-35: 1. b. iv; 2. a. ii; 3. d. iii; 4. c. i; 5. g. viii; 6. h. v; 7. f. vii; 8. e. vi

Page 36-37: 1. Badminton; 2. Quidditch; 3. Football; 4. Tennis; 5. Hockey; 6. Golf; 7. Table Tennis; 8. Basketball; 9. Tennis; 10. Football; 11. Quidditch; 12. Hockey; 13. Golf; 14. Basketball; 15. Table Tennis; 16. Badminton

Page 38: 1. e; 2. j; 3. a; 4. f; 5. b; 6. i; 7. d; 8. g; 9. h; 10. c

Page 39: 1. Neurologist; 2. Paediatrician; 3. Cardiologist; 4. Psychiatrist; 5. Dentist; 6. Surgeon; 7. Opthalmologist; 8. Dermatologist

Page 40-41 1. Kashmir; 2. Rajasthan; 3. Goa; 4. Karnataka; 5. Himachal Pradesh; 6. Bihar; 7. Assam; 8. Punjab; 9. Maharashtra

Page 42-43 1. b; 2. d; 3. e; 4. c; 5. a; 6. g; 7. i; 8. j; 9. h; 10. f

Page 44: 1. F; 2. T; 3. F; 4. F; 5. F; 6. F; 7. T; 8. F; 9. T; 10. F; 11. F; 12. F; 13. T; 14. T; 15. F; 16. T

Page 45: 1. e; 2. g; 3. i; 4. j; 5. h; 6. b; 7. c; 8. a; 9. d; 10. f

Page 46: 1. f; 2. c; 3. e; 4. b; 5. a; 6. h; 7. d; 8. g

Page 47: 1. False; 2. True; 3. True; 4. False; 5. True; 6. True; 7. False; 8. False

Page 48-49: 1. Globe; 2. Medical syringe; 3. Mindshield wiper; 4. Life raft; 5. Submarine telescope; 6. Car heater; 7. Fire escape; 8. Electric water heater; 9. Home security system; 10. Roti maker

Page 50: 1. Sawai Jai Singh II, Jantar Mantar, Amer; 2. Hawa Mahal, *jaalis;* 3. Gayatri Devi, blue pottery; 4. Foot; 5. Lit Fest

Page 51: 1. c; 2. d; 3. f; 4. a; 5. b; 6. e

Page 52-53: 1. 380001; 2. 600001; 3. 751001; 4. 171001; 5. 302001; 6. 791111; 7. 737101; 8. 226001; 9. 560002; 10. 744101

Page 54-55: 1. Vikram Sarabhai; 2. C.V Raman; 3. Har Gobind Khorana; 4. Homi Bhaba; 5. Salim Ali; 6. Jagadish Chandra Bose; 7. Meghnad Saha; 8. Satyendra Nath Bose

Page 56-57: 1. trees, carbon dioxide, 2. greenhouse; 3. energy, gases; 4. energy; 5. heating; 6. water, energy; 7. bulbs; 8. socket; 9. public, 10. warming

Page 58-59:

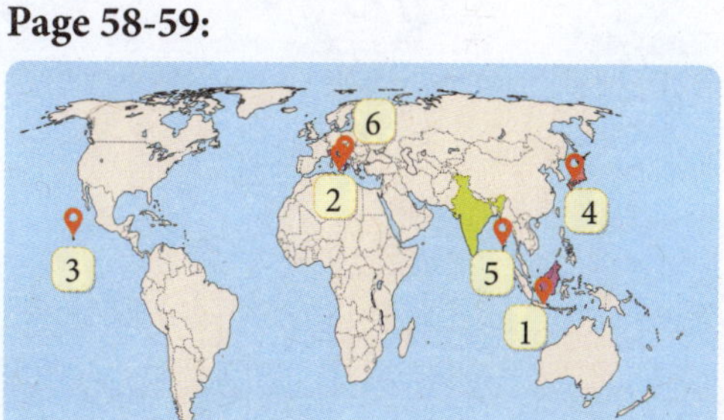

1. Indonesia; 2. Italy; 3. Hawaii; 4. Japan; 5. Andaman and Nicobar Islands; 6. Southern Italy

Page 60-61: 1. Madhubani, 2. Miniature, 3. Warli, 4. Pahari, 5. Tanjore

Page 62-63: 1. cricket; 2. golf; 3. boxing; 4. swimming; 5. gymnastics; 6. basketball; 7. football; 8. athletics; 9. hockey; 10. tennis

Page 64-65: 2. shell, walk, gills; 3. bird, Bones, feathers, fly, lungs, land; 4. water, mammals, lungs, swim, Bones, hair; 5. amphibians, land, water, hop, swim; 6. reptiles, scales, land, lungs, crawl; 7. reptile, land, water, bones, scales, lungs, crawls; 8. swims, Bones, scales, gills

Page 66: 1. Annie Besant; 2. Lakshmi Sahgal; 3. Kasturba Gandhi; 4. Kamaladevi Chattopadhyay; 5. Rani Lakshmibai; 6. Begum Hazrat Mahal; 7. Sarojini Naidu; 8. Aruna Asaf Ali

Page 67: 1. (✓); 2. (×); 3. (✓); 4. (×); 5. (✓); 6. (×); 7. (✓); 8. (✓); 9. (×); 10. (×); 11. (×); 12. (✓)

1. English and Tamil; 2. Address

Page 68-69: 1. *Kathputli;* 2. *Tholu Bommalata;* 3. *Putul Nautch;* 4. *Kathikundei Nach;* 5. *Pavakoothu;* 6. *Gombeyatta;* 7. *Kalasutri bahulya;* 8. *Kundhei*

Page 70-71: 1. e; 2. d; 3. f; 4. c; 5. b; 6. a; 7. h; 8. i; 9. g

Page 72: 1. Afghanistan; 2. 2 cm; 3. Siachen; 4. Antarctica; 5. Sir Andrew Waugh; 6. Tenzing Norgay; 7. Dhaulagiri; 8. roof of the world

Page 73: 1. Taj Mahal Palace; 2. King George V; 3. Queen Mary; 4. George Wittet; 5. Apollo Bunder; 6. Elephanta Island

Page 74: 1. Jahangir Khan; 2. sugarcane; 3. footballs; 4. markhor; 5. Gwadar Port; 6. Shandur Pass; 7. Karachi; 8. Changa Manga; 9. jasmine; 10. Ansoo; 11. Islamabad; 12. chukar partridge; 13. blind dolphin; 14. Tharparkar

Page 75: 1. Sriharikota; 2. Mangalyaan; 3. Kalpana Chawla; 4. Aryabhatta; 5. Chandrayaan-1; 6. Rakesh Sharma

Page 76: 1. c; 2. a; 3. h; 4. b; 5. d; 6. f; 7. e; 8. g

Page 77: 1. Field Marshal; 2. Admiral; 3. Air Marshal; 4. Rear Admiral; 5. Brigadier;

6. Colonel; 7. Wing Commander; 8. Squadron Leader; 9. Captain; 10. Sub-Lieutenant

Page 78-79: 1. Kurds; 2. Romani; 3. Rohingya; 4. Uyghur; 5. Tibetans; 6. Inuit; 7. Basque; 8. Tuareg

Page 80-81: 1. humans; 2. functional; 3. environments; 4. survivors; 5. Czech; 6. unimate; 7. bots; 8. Isaac Asimov

Quiz Yourself 1: 1. c; 2. b; 3. d; 4. b; 5.a; 6. d; 7. b; 8. b; 9. c; 10. a.

Quiz Yourself 2: 1. c; 2. a; 3. b; 4. c; 5.a; 6. c; 7.a; 8. b; 9. c; 10. d

Quiz Yourself 3: 1. a; 2. d; 3. c; 4. d; 5.a; 6. d; 7. b; 8. a; 9. c; 10. b

Quiz Yourself 4: 1. a; 2. d; 3. a; 4. b; 5.c; 6. b; 7.a; 8. c; 9. a; 10. b